...orrupted from the simplicity that is in Christ... For Satan transforms himself

...ansform themselves into ministers of righteousness..." -2 Corinthians 11:3,14

SCIENCE
THE SUPPRESSED EVIDENCE

BRUCE A. MALONE

"For the wrath of God is revealed from heaven against all ungodliness and unrighteousness of men, who suppress the truth in unrighteousness, because what may be known of God is manifest... for since the creation of the world His invisible attributes are clearly seen, being understood by the things that are made..." -Romans 1:18-20

Search for the Truth Publications
3255 Monroe Rd. Midland, MI 48642
(989) 837-5546
Web - www.searchforthetruth.net
Email - truth@searchforthetruth.net

Cover Design - Michael Malone & Shelley Mordue
Graphic Artists – Michael Malone, Shelley Mordue, & Jill Gerhardt
All Scripture References from New King James Holy Bible

ISBN: 978-0-9715911-5-8 (Hardcover)
Library of Congress Control Number: 2009905438
Expanded and revised fourth printing - November 2014
Revised Fifth Printing - October 2021

Printed in China

Search for the Truth Publication Policy:

God's Word has triumphed over every effort to discredit and distort its reliability for thousands of years. There are FAR more ancient Bible manuscripts than for any other historical document and these manuscripts agree with modern verbatim translations word for word. It is clear that the Bible is a unique and incredibly accurate historic book.

A primary function of our publications is to demonstrate how well facts from both history and science fit a straightforward Biblical framework of reality. Factual errors occasionally creep into any book, however, there is never an excuse for distorting the truth to fit one's bias. Christianity and the Bible have nothing to fear from an honest evaluation of the truth. Please contact us if any of the information found within Search for the Truth Publications is factually incorrect in any way. It is our policy to remove or correct any factual errors in subsequent printings.

DEDICATION

In memory of my mother, Margaret Rose Malone, who had the faith of a child and did not need evidence from science to know that Jesus was her Creator, Redeemer, and Lord. May this book move others toward such a profound faith.

Censored Science is also dedicated to the memory of my nephew, Jaryd Wellstead Gilts. His is the generation I hope to reach with this book – bringing meaning and purpose that are built upon the reality that we have both a powerful Creator and a loving Savior.

ACKNOWLEDGEMENTS

This book would have little impact without the artistic talents of Michael Malone and Shelley Mordue. These phenomenally gifted and creative designers took my concepts and brought them to life throughout the pages of this book. I am deeply indebted to both of you.

My wife, Robin, has had the patience of a saint as day after day my far-off gaze and silence told her my mind was again occupied with how best to simplify some concept for "The Book." Her support has made this project possible. I love you deeply and always.

My editors and proofreaders turned this rough gemstone into a sparkling diamond. My special gratitude goes to Pam Koehlinger for comments, suggestions, and editing of the entire volume. Thanks to Don, Jeri, & Aaron Slinger, Julie & Vince VonVett, Doug Lee, Kent Larson, Claudia Malone and Stephen B. Austin for proofreading corrections and content suggestions. Thanks to Roger Zakariasen for many improvements to the fifth revised printing.

Thanks to Dr. Steve Austin for technical editing of the geology section; Dr. John Baumgardner for technical editing of the geology and physics sections; Dr. Tim Clarey for technical editing of the geology section; Dr. John Sanford for final technical editing of the biology section. For these brilliant scientists to take time from their busy schedules to review this book is truly an honor.

Thanks also to the many who financially supported and prayed over this project. The list is too long to name everyone involved – your reward will be fully realized in heaven when you meet those touched by your part in this work.

Lastly, thanks to Kent Larson -- the accomplished storyteller -- who taught me that it is truth emphasized by stories, not bare facts, which imparts the most lasting impact.

CONTENTS

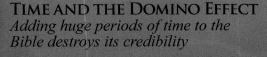

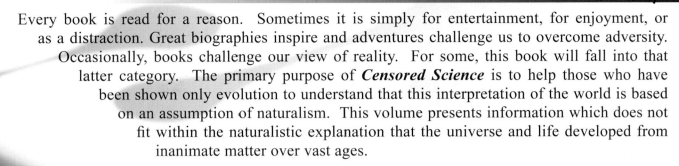

Every book is read for a reason. Sometimes it is simply for entertainment, for enjoyment, or as a distraction. Great biographies inspire and adventures challenge us to overcome adversity. Occasionally, books challenge our view of reality. For some, this book will fall into that latter category. The primary purpose of **Censored Science** is to help those who have been shown only evolution to understand that this interpretation of the world is based on an assumption of naturalism. This volume presents information which does not fit within the naturalistic explanation that the universe and life developed from inanimate matter over vast ages.

Science is currently saturated by the belief that natural causes can explain everything. Yet all data must be interpreted. Observations and evidence cannot reveal truth without being placed within some framework of understanding. No amount of data or information is likely to change someone's mind if their starting assumption is a belief that everything must have a natural cause (i.e. no involvement by God). Even brilliant scientists can be blind to interpretations which do not agree with their presuppositions (starting assumptions). This tendency is as true in understanding scientific truths as with deciding which car looks or performs best. This book simply presents a number of startling observations which fit perfectly into a straightforward understanding of biblical truth but contradict the paradigm of evolution. Thus **Censored Science** provides an "end run" around the blockade of censorship within our education system, which only shows students naturalistic explanations for everything.

The visual imagery of this book is designed to draw the reader to the biblical truths of creation. Each page is akin to a tiny morsel of food, any one of which is unlikely to satisfy the hunger of someone starving for truth, but which, like a succulent appetizer, heightens the sense of hunger. Many pages make reference to phenomenal books that go into much greater technical depth; this is where the full meal can be obtained. Yet even appetizers can satisfy if enough are consumed. Taken as a whole, this book forms a smorgasbord for trusting God's Word as it relates to the real physical world around us.

Censored Science has taken three years from concept to publication, with the goal of making each page a visually stunning masterpiece. I hope those blinded by assumptions of naturalism may come to see the truth; those deafened by apathy will desire to reverberate reality to others; and those lamed by the hopelessness of evolution will walk in the liberation of knowing the Bible can be trusted.

What is Biblical Creation?

Modern science is ruled by an assumption that natural causes must explain everything (naturalism). This assumption is like a rope wrapped around the mind - a rope which prevents those immersed in this viewpoint from interpreting data from biology, geology, and cosmology in light of another possibility - the reality that we have a Creator who has revealed the true history of the universe to us in the Bible.

The Bible provides a clear answer to how, when, and why all of reality came into existence, and there is much scientific data which supports its straightforward statements. Unfortunately, naturalistic assumptions within our schools, museums, and media result in the continued censorship of any evidence which questions the ruling paradigm of evolution.

A formidable number of scientists, ranging from agnostics to Bible-believing Christians, have masterfully presented the biological evidence showing why life could not possibly have formed by natural processes. This movement is known as "intelligent design" and is opposed with a vengeance by those devoted to preventing students from considering anything but natural causes for our existence. Because of the strength of the intelligent design arguments, the binding influence from the rope of biological naturalism is loosening. Yet if God has created life, this event must be placed within a real context of history. How and when did this creation take place? Only a loosening of the binding ropes of geological and cosmological naturalism allows the straightforward understanding of the Bible to be considered.

Scientific evidence and data provide indicators as to whether we came into existence via natural processes plus lots of time, or whether the Bible can be trusted to explain the history of our past in a straightforward way. The implications are huge. Either God created life, or natural processes over lengthy time periods created life. Either there have been enormous periods of time which created the geologic record, or the underlying rock was created rapidly and the fossil record is the result of an earth-covering flood. Believing that God used natural processes over huge periods of time is just another way of saying the Bible cannot be trusted to mean what it states in a straightforward way. If this is true, why believe anything the Bible has to say?

There is much evidence which points to something beyond natural causes. This evidence is simply ignored, suppressed, or misinterpreted because it does not fit into the assumptions of naturalism. Yet the implications are so significant that they must be considered and discussed. This book presents a small sample of the scientific observations and evidence which fits perfectly into a biblical model of the recent creation of the universe, earth, life, and the reality of a worldwide flood. ***Censored Science: The Suppressed Evidence*** invites you to consider the evidence related to earth history which is suppressed by our education system because of the binding influence of naturalism.

COSMOLOGICAL NATURALISM

A Note About SKEPTIC'S CORNER

This book contains some of the most compelling scientific evidences supporting biblical Creation. Yet evidence itself can always be interpreted in more than one way. For this reason, each page contains a section called the "*Skeptic's Corner.*"

Evidence supporting supernatural creation, a worldwide flood, and divine providence seem to be particularly repugnant to modern intellectuals. For this reason very few people are ever exposed to the actual evidences supporting creation. At best they are shown "straw man" distortions of the creation evidence. The straw man approach presents a distortion of creation researcher conclusions and then attacks the distortion in order to discredit those who reject naturalistic evolution as an explanation for the existence of the world.

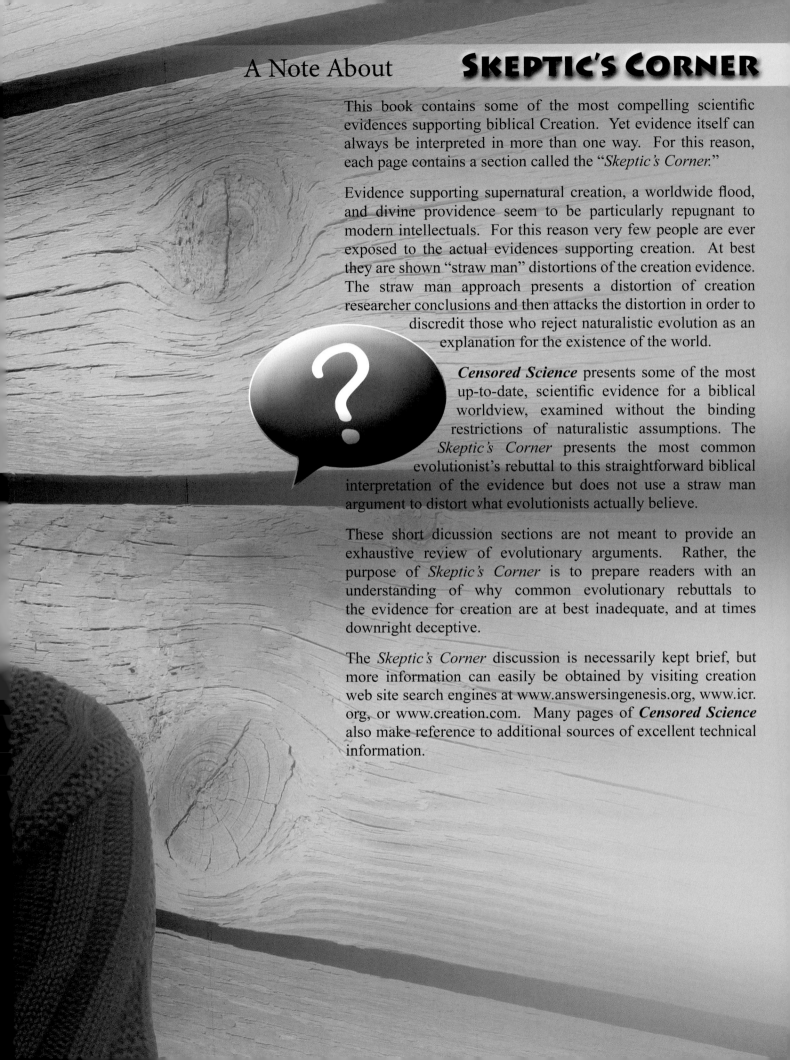

Censored Science presents some of the most up-to-date, scientific evidence for a biblical worldview, examined without the binding restrictions of naturalistic assumptions. The *Skeptic's Corner* presents the most common evolutionist's rebuttal to this straightforward biblical interpretation of the evidence but does not use a straw man argument to distort what evolutionists actually believe.

These short dicussion sections are not meant to provide an exhaustive review of evolutionary arguments. Rather, the purpose of *Skeptic's Corner* is to prepare readers with an understanding of why common evolutionary rebuttals to the evidence for creation are at best inadequate, and at times downright deceptive.

The *Skeptic's Corner* discussion is necessarily kept brief, but more information can easily be obtained by visiting creation web site search engines at www.answersingenesis.org, www.icr.org, or www.creation.com. Many pages of *Censored Science* also make reference to additional sources of excellent technical information.

CENSORED BIOLOGY

We have all been conditioned to believe that it is the step-by-step addition of parts which has transformed non-life to living organisms and simple organisms into more complex creatures. Although this was proposed by Charles Darwin over 150 years ago, there remain many unanswered questions concerning this belief:

How could a half-formed feature survive while the rest of the 'new feature' is yet to evolve? Why isn't every creature full of leftover (now useless) features from the previous forms of life from which it evolved?

Why have scientists, even using advanced equipment and pre-existing chemicals, not come remotely close to producing life in a lab? Why is life via random reactions essentially impossible even if every subatomic particle could have interacted with every other subatomic particle every nanosecond for billions of years?

Mutations are "copying errors" which always destroy some existing information (like rearranging a few letters in a book with each printing). What keeps these seemingly insignificant, tiny changes from gradually building up over time to destroy the information content within the DNA molecule?

Why is the ape-to-man lineage so controversial and ever-changing - even amongst avid evolutionists? Why is the linkage from ape to man not more clear-cut?

How could single cells have turned into starfish, plankton, coral, fish, clams, nautiloids, trilobites, jellyfish, and a host of other incredibly diverse and complex forms of life without leaving any transitional forms between these vastly dissimilar creatures?

These and many more biological questions will be explored in this section. When Charles Darwin proposed the concept of evolution, the 'simple cell' was believed to be no more complex that a small blob of jelly. With the advent of the electron microscope and other tools of modern science, the cell has come to be acknowledged as more complex than any modern chemical manufacturing plant. A biblical understanding of biology is critical to unraveling the strangling influence of biological naturalism, which in turn allows us to consider possibilities other than evolution as the correct explanation for our existence.

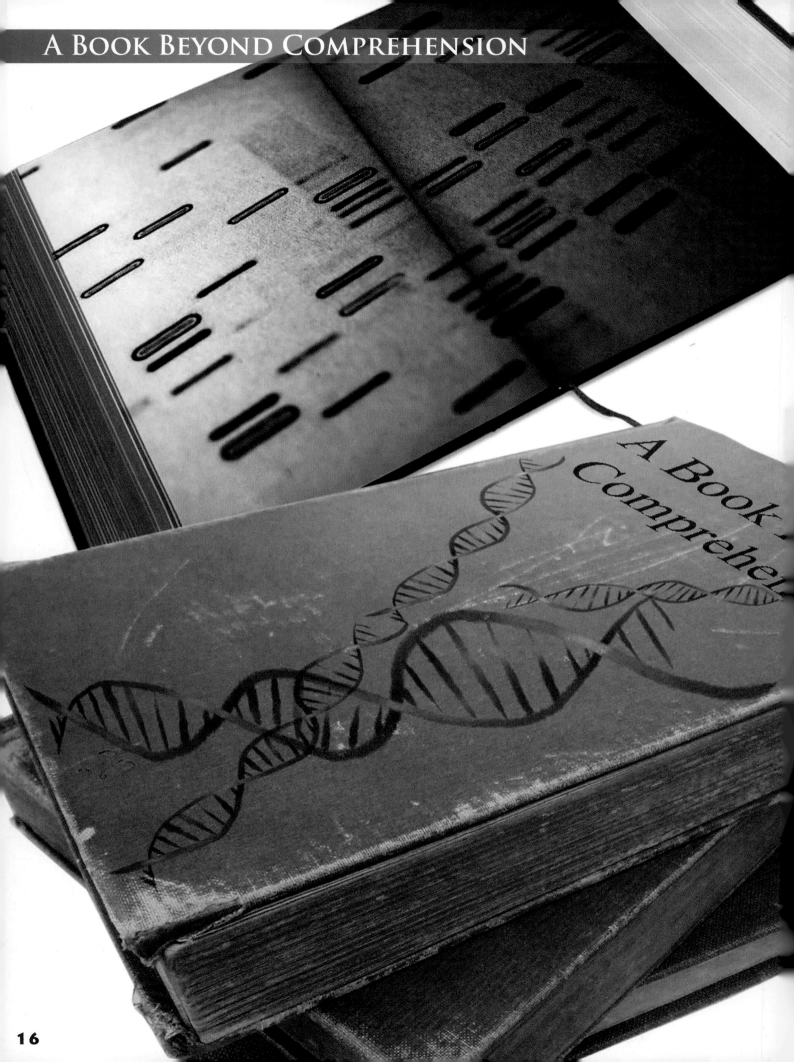

Imagine reading a great *mystery novel* which kept you enthralled until the very last page. You were so excited that you couldn't wait to share the book with a close colleague from Germany. After reading the book he complimented you on the great book *on the history of Europe* which was written in German. He said he enjoyed it so much that he passed it on to a friend from Spain. When you went to retrieve it a week later, the Spaniard stated it was a *fantastic adventure* which he had given to his mother-in-law (of French origin) and he was surprised to find the "excellent book" written in perfect Spanish. Thoroughly confused, you immediately go to visit his inlaw but she was so enthralled by the *"French romance"* that she finished it in one evening and passed it on to her husband who worked at the Department of Defense. She stated that he had taken the book to work because he had never seen such a book in which every sentence could be read either *"forwards or backwards"* and still make perfect sense. Everyone involved would be in **absolute awe** of the incomprehensible genius of an author who could pen such a versatile work.

DNA is exactly such a book.[1] Yet every biology department at every public university in the world is busy training students to believe that this marvelous wonder "wrote itself".

Recent discoveries in DNA analysis have proven that overlapping parts of the same "letter" sequence along the DNA code are used to produce completely different protein molecules. Other studies have shown that DNA letter sequences can produce different proteins if read forward verse being decoded from the same area backwards. This is similar to a book in which the same sentences can be read in completely different languages, read forward or backwards, and give different yet completely clear meanings. Now imagine how such a book could have developed by some random process of letter rearrangement. It becomes immediately apparent that such a book could never have developed in this random, change-one-letter-at-a-time fashion. It had to have been written by an entity of incomprehensible genius. This is the image we should comprehend of God when we truly understand what he has created in the DNA molecule.

1. ***Biological Information: New Perspectives***, edited by Robert Marks,et.al., "Multiple overlapping genetic codes profoundly reduce the probability of beneficial mutation", Robert Marks, World Scientific Publishing, 2013.

SKEPTIC'S ? CORNER

Science has become short-sighted by only considering natural processes for the development of life (i.e. "life made itself", "the DNA code wrote itself", etc.) Therefore, biologists are forced to accept that sometime in the past, random rearrangements of the DNA code produced useful proteins (i.e., a "readable sentence" in this analogy). They then assume that because the new protein was useful, the code for this protein became permanently fixed upon the DNA molecule, and this code would be passed onto further generations. Given their belief in an almost infinite time frame, it is hard to argue that this is not at least possible. BUT try to explain how this sentence (i.e. the DNA coding) could have developed by random changes and be comprehensible in other languages, or backwards, and also make perfect sense each step along the way. During the random development of this sentence, any letter which was changed would have to not interfere with, or destroy, the meaning of any of the other sentences in other languages already coded into the sentence! It is simply impossible for random chance processes (such as mutations) to achieve this level of complexity.

As humans have come to understand the true complexity of the DNA code, it has become nonsensical to believe it "wrote itself". God has made it absolutely apparent that he is the one who created every component of life. It is both an insidious tragedy and the height of irony that students in our universities are not allowed to even consider this possibility.

Wagons and Space Shuttles

Can evolution explain upward advancement in complexity? This is the key question for determining whether evolution is a viable scientific tool or just the foundational dogma of an atheistic worldview. This is how evolution is supposed to work:

A simple creature makes a "copying mistake" or gets zapped by a cosmic ray, resulting in a re-arranging of its DNA information. It is remotely possible that every so often one of these changes may have an effect which will help the organism survive better. If so, that creature will make more surviving copies of itself than the creature which does not have the change (i.e. natural selection will preferentially select the creature with this new advantage). Multiply this effect over billions of creatures for billions of years and, voila, we've turned pond slime into people.

These copying mistakes are very similar to moving a few letters in a 1,000-page novel. The information content of even the simplest form of life is so enormous that even though these changes are consistently negative, the effect upon any one generation is essentially unnoticeable - like biological noise. The change to one generation would be like a few thousand atoms of rust upon your car, not yet visible, but still there and spreading.

Let's examine how this explanation for life's upward development withstands closer scrutiny. Suppose I had a little red wagon and wanted to turn it into a space shuttle. If the wagon were a simple cell, attached to each wagon would be the manufacturing specifications needed to construct the next wagon. (This would be like the DNA code.) By making random changes to the wagon's manufacturing instructions, could a wagon manufacturing facility eventually start turning out space shuttles? Obviously not. This is an excellent visual analogy of the impossibility of random mutational changes turning a single-celled organism into a person.

But what about natural selection?

Now imagine the wagon manufacturing manual has 10,000 pages with 1000 letters per page and that each manual must explain every part of the manufacturing facility. That manual would be about two hundred times thicker than this book. If we were to randomly change 100 of the ten million letters in this manual, it is VERY unlikely to affect our ability to produce useable wagons. 99.99+ percent of the changes would be unnoticeable even though

18

information was being destroyed. Natural selection is analogous to the quality control department - it can only see changes to the finished wagon, not changes to the manufacturing manual. But think about what happens with subsequent generations: The next generation of wagons has 100 more random mistakes - we now have 200 permanent detrimental changes. In only 100 generations we have built up 10,000 permanent random changes. (One percent of the total instructions have now become garbled.)

At some point more and more wagons have to be rejected because they no longer function properly. Even if an occasional wagon "generation" sells better, it takes with it all the deleterious random changes which have built up to this point and will ultimately continue to deteriorate downwards. Will the wagon ever turn into a space shuttle? NO! **This is reality.** In the same way, random mutations filtered by natural selection may separate variations within different "kinds" of creatures, but they will never transform one type of creature into a completely new type of complex organism.

Natural selection cannot cause an increase in information complexity; it merely filters the information already present. Changes to the DNA code from one generation to the next (called birth defects and genetic diseases in humans) are not driving simple life to increasing complexity, but ultimately driving all life toward extinction. This increasing load of genetic mistakes is a result of the fallen nature of all creation. The speed at which these mistakes are building up is one of the primary evidences that no form of life on earth could be millions of years old.[1]

[1]*Genetic Entropy and the Mystery of the Genome*, Dr. J.C. Sanford, FMS Publications, 2005.

SKEPTIC'S CORNER

This is one of those areas where the style of the response is more revealing than the words chosen. When presented with the concept of Genetic Entropy (downward deterioration of information on the genome), skeptics respond by avoiding the primary issue. You see lots of examples of variation of information within a given type of creature, but how complex new information could develop (i.e. new creatures, new organs, or even major changes to existing features) is not addressed in any substantive way. This avoidance of the real issue is actually a subtle acknowledgement of the strength of this evidence for our recent creation.

The biological world is an awe-inspiring, wonder-filled marvel to behold. It is also the best cure for atheism, because the design of nature is so apparent. So how do atheists maintain their belief in design without a designer in face of the evidence from living organisms? Those wishing to explain life's wonders without God use evolution as their foundation for explaining everything. In other words, they believe that small changes over huge periods of time produced the wonders of nature. But is this true?

One of the principal observations which fly in the face of this belief is the interdependence of various functions of any organism. On a molecular level this principle has been called *irreducible complexity*, because for most biological features to function there is a minimum number of parts or steps which must be present.

Take, for example, the clotting of blood. Imagine designing a fluid which must flow like water through minute

tubes (capillaries) but once exposed to oxygen must rapidly thicken to the point that the flow stops, even with relatively high pressure forcing the fluid out of the exposed opening in the tubing. For blood to perform this function it goes through seventeen specifically designed reactions to form a network of clotted solids which seal off a cut. If any of these seventeen steps is missing (any component of any reaction) or any of the reactions is out of sequence, the blood thickens too soon or too late. Either way, you die. This sequence of events displays *irreducible complexity*. Everything must be present, in the right order, and in the right place, or nothing works. But how did all the right parts or reactions develop in the first place?

An analogy might be a simple mouse trap. The mouse trap has only five basic parts - the base, the hammer, the catch, the spring, and the hold-down lever. Yet if any of these parts is missing the trap will never function properly. You could even put exactly the right five parts in a can and shake, spin, twirl, drop, or explode the can for five billion years, but a working mouse trap would never result. For the mouse trap to work each part needs to be in the right position and performing the right function. The same is true for the clotting of blood and all of life on both a molecular and a macro scale.[1]

The chameleon provides another example of this interwoven complexity of parts. There are about ninety species of chameleon (fifty-nine in Madagascar alone), and all likely developed from one or two originally created "kinds."

Chameleons have the ability to see in two opposite directions at once while independently focusing and accurately judging the distance to both extremely close and extremely distant objects. These independent, roving, telephoto eyes are uniquely associated with the chameleon kind. This ability is needed in order to accurately shoot their incredibly-designed tongue at their prey.

The chameleon's tongue can be up to 1½ times the length of its body and is attached to a special catapulting bone structure which allows it to be launched with an acceleration of fifty g's (fifty times the acceleration experienced by a falling object). Test pilots pass out at an acceleration of approximately ten g's. No other vertebrate has muscles capable of movement this fast. This tongue/catapult structure is unique in the animal kingdom, with no known ancestral linkage to any similar structure.[2] But even this would be useless if the tongue were not capable of grabbing onto its prey. Two muscles pull the front of the tongue inward just before the tongue strikes the prey, forming a suction cup. It took special super-high-speed photographic techniques even to discover how all these mechanisms work in concert to allow this unique organism to survive.

It is theoretically possible to make up a story of how the chameleon's specialized eyes, tongue, and catapult structures all just happened to develop independently in order to work perfectly in concert. But given that there is no fossil evidence of any other creatures possessing such structures, it would seem to be a more logical conclusion that the features were created all at the same time, rather than developed by many small step-changes over huge periods of time.

Darwin's Black Box: The Biochemical Challenge to Evolution, Michael Behe, Free Press, 1998.

"Catapults' give chameleon tongues superspeed, Trivedi, B.P., <news. nationalgeographic.com/news/2004/05/0519_040519_tvchameleons. html>, 19 May 2004.

Canned Life

Can random reactions transform simple molecules into the complex compounds needed for life to develop from chemicals? We have all been conditioned to believe that it is the step-by-step addition of parts which has transformed non-life to living organisms and simple organisms into more complex creatures. Yet after a hundred years of laboratory trials we are as close to discovering how chemicals could "come alive" as someone scaling Mt. Everest would be from the top after moving the width of a hair from their base camp.

The Urey-Miller experiment, first conceived in 1953, remains the closest attempt at showing how simple chemicals (methane, ammonia, hydrogen and water) could be transformed into the more complex amino acids which form the basic structure of living organisms. Yet this experiment did not produce all of the amino acids needed for life, used laboratory conditions not found anywhere in the natural world, did not use oxygen (which other evidence indicates has always existed in earth's atmosphere), and resulted in a detrimental/biologically-useless mixture of chemicals. What this highly exalted experiment actually proved is that life could not possibly have formed in this way. Yet it is still found in textbooks as evidence for evolution because nothing better has come along.

Let's pretend that by some miraculous event every chemical structure which is needed to form the first living, reproducing cell somehow miraculously appeared. The problems with life forming from those chemicals would STILL be insurmountable. For instance:

- How would the chemicals find each other? The correct organic molecules formed in a test tube would be unbelievably dispersed and statistically unlikely to react in the proper sequence. The same chemicals formed in some pond or ocean would never connect.

- How could the "right" chemicals be kept from having the "wrong" reactions? The chemicals of life are extremely complex and fragile. For instance, DNA formation is a reversible reaction in water, and DNA rapidly 'unzips' when placed in water. Yet life was supposed to have formed in water. A living cell has numerous mechanisms to protect DNA from degradation, but outside of a cell these degradation reactions occur millions of times more rapidly than the reactions needed to form such a useful biological structure.

- It is possible to place millions of the simplest form of a life (such as bacteria) into the bottom of a test tube and physically split open their cell membranes. This allows all of the life-giving chemicals to spill out into the bottom of the test tube. At that moment all of the right chemicals, in exactly the right proportions, at exactly the right temperature, are present at the bottom of the test tube. Yet no living organism has resulted from this perfect combination of chemicals.

- How did the first cell come to life and then learn to reproduce copies of itself? From where did the 350,000 to 500,000 DNA code pairs within a "simple" cell come? How did they come together in the right order to direct cell division – all while the cell continued to perform other needed functions to exist?

Another "formation of life experiment" has been performed over a billion times a year for the last hundred years. This experiment combines all of the needed chemicals required by life inside of an open thermodynamic container (one which allows heat and sometimes light to pass in and out of the chemical soup). Yet, not once in the hundred billion times that this experiment has been run has any new form of life appeared. This experiment is called "canned food." Everything from canned tuna to preserved vegetables contain all of the chemicals needed for life to form, in a far more purified form than any random laboratory experiment could ever produce, yet no new critter has ever crawled out of your can of pineapples. And you can thank the Lord that as long as the ingredients are properly sterilized, it never will.

SKEPTIC'S CORNER

Naturalism simply cannot explain life's origin. The Miller-Urey experiment is still promoted in high school and college textbooks as an explanation for how life could have developed - in spite of the fact that the results of this experiment are always a mixture of relatively useless chemicals essentially poisonous to life. Recently there was great fanfare as bits of nucleic acid placed in a test tube were shown to be spontaneously surrounded by fatty molecules in a laboratory experiment. Yet this is no more amazing than a bit of fat being surrounded by a soap molecule while washing dishes in your kitchen sink. The very fact that such irrelevant experiments continue to be promoted is a testimony to how little progress evolutionary scientists have made toward explaining the formation of life.

Nutrition Facts

Serving Size 2 slices (114g)
Servings Per Container about 3

Amount Per Serving

	Calories from Fat 0
Calories 60	

% Daily Value

Total Fat 0g

Sodium 10mg

Potassium 105mg

Total Carbohydrate 14g

Dietary Fiber 1g

Sugars 13g

"Diets rich in fruits & vegetables may reduce the risk of some types of cancer and other chronic diseases."
— National Cancer Institute

Freaky Frogs

Two of the most diverse forms of life on our planet are frogs and toads. Scientists have named over 4,800 distinct groups (species) of these amphibians, which have a dizzying array of appearances and abilities. Southeast Asian frogs have flaps of skin between their toes that enable them to glide. The wood frog allows up to two-thirds of its body to freeze in the winter with its heart, breathing, and kidneys shut down for months. The Surinam toad absorbs eggs into honeycomb-like chambers within its skin, where they remain for twenty weeks before emerging as young frogs. Not to be outdone, the Australian aquatic frog eats its eggs, then shuts down its stomach acids to form an incubator for the young; eight weeks later fullgrown frogs crawl out of the mother's mouth. The gold-banded arrow-poison frog produces poison so toxic that just touching an arrow or dart to its skin gathers enough poison on the tip to instantly kill a man shot by the arrow.

There are frogs which have the ability to regurgitate their entire stomach, should they accidentally eat a poisonous substance. Once the stomach is outside its body, the frog wipes away the undesirable food and swallows its stomach again! Frogs typically eat by catching insects in mid-air; yet most species have relatively short tongues. This problem is overcome by the fact that their tongues are backwards – attached at the front of the mouth instead of the back, where most vertebrates' tongues are attached. Most frogs have the ability to breathe both through their skin and using their lungs, while some species have extremely complex and specialized features which even extract oxygen directly from water.

New species of frogs and toads are still being discovered (recently 200 new species were identified in Madagascar and 100 in Sri Lanka). Sometimes these discoveries take place in the most unexpected places. In 1853, General Darius Nash Couch took a one-year leave of absence from the army to conduct a scientific mission for the Smithsonian Institute and happened upon a dried lake bed in Northern Mexico when it started to rain. To his amazement, thousands of toads suddenly popped out of the dry desert soil. These creatures spend up to a year lying dormant underground, waiting to hear the drumming of raindrops on the soil. As soon as it rains (often only once a year) the males search out a newly formed pool, and their chorus draws the silent females to them.

Their tadpoles must hatch, grow, and change into toadlets before the pool evaporates in the summer sun. Named the Couch's spadefoot toads, the toadlets sometimes leave the puddle only nine days after being an egg. They are voraciously hungry, devouring everything in sight, including algae off rocks, and filtering microorganisms from the water that they pump over their gills. They then disappear underground for another year of waiting for rain.

Hundreds of beneficial chemicals have been extracted from frogs. One biochemical substance produced by amphibian skin is a highly effective painkiller, which is two hundred times stronger than morphine but not as addictive. Green tree frog skin secretions have been shown to stimulate activity in the human pancreas and intestine, and commercial drugs are now available based on these compounds. The glands located just behind the eyes of certain frogs have produced substances that aid functions of the adrenal and cardiovascular systems in humans. Frog skin secretions can also have powerful antibiotic properties. The skin of the African clawed frog produces proteins that have been shown to speed the healing of cuts and bruises.

How did this laundry list of amazing functions and features, chemicals and compounds, abilities and advantages come about? There are only two possibilities. Either they are the creation of an unfathomably imaginative designer OR some previous non-frog-like creature turned into the first frog, which then turned into all the other types of frogs and toads. If the second possibility (evolution) is true, then at every step along the way the transforming frog must have had some sort of advantage, or the partial creature would never have survived. How did a mother frog learn to turn off its stomach acids to provide a nest and then swallow its young? How did a frog learn to produce poisons without killing itself first? How did a frog learn to freeze its heart in order to survive the first frozen winter? How did toads learn to live underground for up to a year and know to come out into the scorching sun only when it starts to rain?

Every one of these remarkable abilities involves hundreds, if not thousands, of specifically designed chemicals, reactions, and bits of useful information coded onto each creature's DNA structure. It could not possibly have just appeared by some random step-by-step additive process resulting in a new function or feature, followed by the ability or instinct necessary to use the newly developed function or feature. The features and abilities exhibited by the fabulous variety of frogs and toads is a convincing testimony to the reality that all of life has a Creator.

DEATH WISH

The most influential and brilliant scientists of the nineteenth and twentieth centuries - Charles Darwin and Albert Einstein – both rejected the existence of a real, personal, Biblical God in favor of a non-intrusive "god" who just started things rolling. Their god was an impersonal force who let nature run its course and was powerless to intervene. Why did these intelligent men come to such a conclusion?

Charles Darwin totally rejected any faith in a Biblical deity after the death of his beloved ten-year-old daughter, Annie, in 1851. Albert Einstein lived during the bloodiest century of all human history - witnessing the mass murder of 6 million Jewish people under Hitler's "final solution" to purifying mankind. Both Einstein and Darwin formed their view of God based on an assumption that God was responsible for death. In Einstein's words, *"[If God made us] he is the one ultimately responsible for our actions...he is behind the harm we do each other. God himself is the source of the very evil he supposedly judges...Free will is an illusion. When science has probed the depths of the human mind, I am convinced we will find the laws that govern it, just like everything else."* [1]

In other words, this is their progression of thought: a) If God made everything, he must also have made death & disease, or be powerless to stop it. b) If he made things this way, then God is evil. If God could prevent evil/death and fails to do so, then God must also be evil. c) Since God cannot be evil, he simply must not exist - or - he must be some sort of "impersonal ordering force" indistinguishable from the natural laws of the universe.

Both Einstein and Darwin understood that a perfect, infinitely powerful Creator must, by definition, be perfectly just. Therefore, sin and evil must be judged. Yet this totally powerful creator must have Himself created the very evil He then must judge. Thus they were caught in a logical dichotomy which caused them to reject a biblical God. What they failed to understand was that God is also the embodiment of infinite mercy and that death

SKEPTIC'S CORNER

Skeptics reject the Bible as a source of knowledge. Therefore, they have to explain death and defense mechanisms without God. To skeptics, the defense mechanisms of insects are not a picture of God's mercy in a fallen world but a result of natural selection. In other words, those creatures with the best defense mechanisms survive best. This is obvious, but how did they develop? How did a beetle develop the programming to look like a thorn, leaf, or stick? How did insects learn to play dead? How did the cellular structure of a butterfly learn to mimic the eyes of an owl? How did one insect learn to mix and shoot hot gases at predators while another mixes toxic, nasty tasting chemicals which harms predators but not itself? Once in place, all of these defense mechanisms are quite useful, but each require thousands of chemical/structural changes – each change working in perfect concert. It is pure fantasy to believe that they developed by small mutational changes, one-step-at-a-time, with every change along the way yielding some useful intermediate creature.

did not start until our actions caused the entire universe to become warped. It is the perfect mercy of God which provides a way back into fellowship with Him.

Both men fell into this faulty view of God by assuming that the Bible does not reveal the true history of our planet. In actuality, the first chapters of the Bible clearly state that it is mankind, not God, who is responsible for every death, problem, and disease within the universe. Mankind chose to rebel against God rather than obey Him. This rebellion did not take God by surprise, because He had created man with the freedom of choice. There would be no free will if there were not the option to choose. When we rejected God's authority, we separated ourselves from God. God then allowed death to enter into creation so that we would not live for eternity separated from our perfect and holy maker. God then set into action a plan to become human and take the death penalty which we deserve upon Himself.

Thus the nature of God is both totally just and totally loving (requiring death for rebellion - which taints all of creation - but providing mercy in the midst of it). This can be seen in the most unlikely of places – such as the insect world. The pain and groaning of creation is as close as the next disease-tainted mosquito stab, painful wasp sting, or poisonous spider bite. But the mercy of God is also apparent from observing the world of insects. One of the great unsolved mysteries of evolutionism is the enormous variety of insect defense mechanisms:

- Insects which look exactly like the twigs, leaves, and thorns upon which they live.
- Insects that prominently display spots which look like the eyes of various preditors.
- Brightly colored insects which have nasty-tasting chemical flavors.
- Insects with loosely connected limbs which break off and twitch when attacked.
- Insects which shoot hot gases at predators.
- Others which roll over and play dead when approached.

The development of any of these defense mechanisms cannot be explained by slow evolutionary changes - they only work because they are fully developed - along with the instincts allowing insects to use their defense mechanisms.

Both Darwin and Einstein missed God because they rejected Genesis as real history and therefore blamed God for a disease-tainted creation. Death is mankind's responsibility. Knowing the penalty for rejecting God's love and mercy, we choose to disobey him anyway. In essence, Adam and Eve had a death wish and brought that penalty upon all of creation. But God illustrates his mercy with actions as sacrificial as taking the death penalty upon himself and as compassionate as providing the unbelievable array of defense mechanisms for the lowly insect in a fallen creation.

1. *Albert Einstein: Out of my Later Years: The Scientist, Philosopher, and the Man Portrayed through His Own Words* (Princeville, Ore.: Bonanza Books, 1990), 30-33; *and Albert Einstein: The World as I See It*, trans. Alan Harris (New York: Citadel Press, 1995), 24-29.

Our Complex Ear

Student teams at MIT are given near-impossible engineering projects and will work for countless hours implementing novel technological solutions to these complex problems. Yet the accomplishments of these brilliant students pale in comparison to even the most routine functions performed by any human organ. The act of hearing is one such function. Suppose this team of engineering experts, given unlimited talent, time, funding, and expertise were assigned the following task: Design a sound detection system which is so accurate that it could detect the sound of a mosquito flying 100 feet from the detector while a freight train, blowing its whistle, is passing within one foot of the sound-detecting equipment. The equipment must also be submerged within a cup of water. Should such a detector be built, no one would ever believe it had arisen by random chance mutational processes; yet that is the only model allowed in our schools as an explanation for the far more complex sense of human hearing.

In order for our brains to receive nerve impulses which can be interpreted as various types of sound or language, sound waves (which are transmitted via minute air pressure variations) must pass from air, through the solid bones behind the eardrum, and into nerves (which are essentially a liquid). Yet 99.9% of sound is reflected and lost when passing from air into liquid. In spite of this, humans are capable of detecting sounds as low as four decibels, which corresponds to 10^{-10} atmosphere of pressure. This tiny amount of pressure actually moves the human eardrum a distance approximately equal to 1/10 the diameter of a hydrogen atom (10^{-16} meter); yet at the same time the brain is interpreting this movement (i.e. hearing the noise), red blood cells 10^{-8} meters in diameter are flowing through the living tissue of the ear drum. The difference in size and noise creation is similar to that of a freight train compared to a mosquito; yet our brain can tune out the freight-train-sized interference and hear the mosquito-sized noise!

Every part of the ear is a marvel of engineering foresight and wonder. The outer ear is exactly the right shape to catch and magnify passing sound waves. The ear channel is exactly the right diameter and depth to magnify the resonance frequency of 4,000 kilohertz sound waves (the average wavelength of a human voice), yet too small to allow fingers inside. The ear channel has wax-producing glands to keep moisture from forming mildew inside of the channel, and unlike normal skin which replaces cells vertically, the layer of skin within the ear grows horizontally outward in order to sweep debris from the ear.

The eardrum is attached to one of three tiny bones which are connected by perfectly designed gaskets. These bones transfer the pressure vibrations from the air to a set of tiny snail-shaped liquid channels deep within our skulls and embedded in bone. The design of these three tiny bones magnifies the miniscule movement of the eardrum, and the last stirrup-shaped bone acts like a tiny piston to force liquid within a sealed, snail-shaped structure to spiral up one side of the channel and back out the other side - bulging a flexible gasket in and out at the outlet end. Between the fluid flow up one side of the channel and back down the other side is a third, completely closed channel, with a completely separate liquid surrounding tiny hair-like structures, each one attached to a nerve leading directly to our brains.

As the sound pressure wave passes the ear, it is magnified in the channel, vibrates the eardrum, and moves the bones attached to the drum (which amplifies the noise up to 100 times) before passing the sound into the spiraling liquid within a complex, snail-shaped structure called the cochlea. The eardrum can respond to sounds covering a noise level range of one million to one. If the noise level is too high, the brain stretches a muscle attached to the eardrum to dampen the sound level - like a hand held against a drum head. If any part is missing, hearing becomes impaired or impossible.

How did the brain learn to interpret the electrical signals from the microscopic hairs correctly? Evolutionists simply don't know. From where did the perfectly tuned little bones, which transfer sound from air to liquid without losing sensitivity, come? Evolutionists simply don't know. How did the fluid-filled, snail-like cochlea develop? Evolutionists simply don't know. How can the brain tune out the enormous movement of blood through the eardrum while sensing angstrom-sized pressure pulses? Evolutionists simply don't know. The incredible structure of our ear is sadly attributed to chance mutational processes, rather than to the Designer of this incredible system.

[1]*From Jaw to Ear: Transition Fossil Reveals Ear Evolution in Action*, David Biello, *Scientific American*, p. 29, March 14, 2007

SKEPTIC'S CORNER

Bold claims by evolution believers state that complex structures, such as the three tiniest bones in the human body (commonly known as the ear's hammer, anvil, and stirrup), have developed by gradual evolutionary changes. It is commonly taught that there was a slow sequence of changes which moved bones from the jaw of an ancient reptile into the ear channel of modern humans - as reptiles turned into mammals - which turned into humans.[1] Yet such speculation does not account for how a functioning ear and a functioning jaw could have been maintained (for survival) during this fictional process, nor have the huge leaps between the various transitions been found within the fossil record. Storytelling and presuppositions that molecules-to-man evolution is a fact should never replace careful scientific observation.

MONKEY BUSINESS

"What if we did have an ape ancestry? What if evolution really were true? ... But the Bible tells us we were made by God, according to our kinds [i.e. Adam and Eve were created 'in the beginning']. The Bible would be shown to be a lie. And if the Bible was a lie, God was a liar. But if God was a liar, He wouldn't be God! There would be no God! Nature would be the only God! ... It doesn't matter if it's true or not, this evolution from lower forms of life. If enough people believed it to be true, they would turn their backs on God! They would throw their Bibles, even if figuratively, into the fire!"

- Fictional character Max Busby from The Darwin Conspiracy by James Scott Bell, p. 58-59, 1995

There are only two possibilities for our existence. Either we descended from some prior form of life, which in turn descended from an even more primitive form of life, which descended from some non-living chemicals (from goo to you by way of the zoo) OR humans were created fully functional as human beings.

So how can we know which possibility is the truth? This quandary cannot be solved in a class of philosophy or comparative religion because those disciplines do not deal with the actual physical evidence. Typical science classes start with the assumption that mankind was not created so all evidence must be interpreted within a naturalistic apes-to-man framework. But what has actually been found? Since 1859, there have been an estimated 8,000 bones, fossils, or artifact fragments found in the earth's sedimentary rock layers which are assumed to be part of our ape-to-man ancestral record. This wealth of fossil evidence should certainly show the progression from ape-like ancestor to human if this has, indeed, happened.

Various renditions of these bones and skulls have been artistically arranged in monkey-to-man charts for the last 150 years. Meanwhile, new finds such as the 2009 announcement of the lemur-like animal (nicknamed Ida) routinely claim to "re-write" the story of human evolution (which has become increasingly complex, rather than easier to comprehend). In reality, human evolution is assumed to be a fact, and the fossil fragments are simply lined up to support this belief. But does this lining up of bones prove that monkey-to-man evolution has happened?

Modern humans have an enormous variation in stature (4 to 7 feet), physical appearance (coal black aborigines to lily white Scandinavians), and brain capacity (700 to 2000 cc). It is apparent from the fossil record that

July 13, 2007 - The tallest Chinese human (7'8") with the smallest (2'5")

this human disparity was even larger in the past, with people ranging from "hobbit-like" stature (barely over 3 feet tall) to Neanderthals having a brain capacity of 2200 cc. It is also apparent that fully human skull shapes were more diverse in the past. Some humans had deep set eyes, eyebrow ridges, heavy jaws, and sloped facial characteristics far more pronounced than today. None of this dissimilarity is proof of evolution, but simply of the enormous variety created within the original human gene pool.

Fully human skull fragments are routinely misinterpreted as non-humans and classified as archaic (meaning ancient) homo-sapiens or homo erectus specimens. In other words, most skulls classified as "homo erectus" are simply part of the enormous variation of buried human skulls. Other fossil fragments are clearly extinct variations of ancient apes. Animals such as australopithecines (like the famous Lucy skeleton) were apes which may have had a more upright posture than many modern apes. The strongest evidence that these fossil finds have been misinterpreted is the fact that erectus-type skulls (closely related to a modern human skull) have been found in the same rock layers as australopithecines (Lucy), while other homo erectus skulls have been found right up to contemporary times, along with modern man!

Whenever human activity, artifacts, or fossils are found deep in rock layers where they shouldn't be, the evidence is classified as "non-human." Fully modern human footprints have been found in the same rock layers as Lucy, as have evidences of fully modern human activities (the use of tools, the burial of the dead, etc.) All of this evidence is simply ignored or attributed to man's ape-like ancestors.[1]

In similar fashion, when erectus-like skulls - with "low-end" brain size, eyebrow ridges, or thick jaws - are found in the same rock layers as modern man, these are explained away as human variation, the result of pathological (disease) or environmental causes. Yet similar skulls found in the sediment layers which have been assigned old dates are proclaimed pre-human ancestors.

Why aren't erectus-like skulls found in rocks assigned with old ages also explained as simply the result of human variation, disease, or environmental causes? This blatant inconsistency in the handling of human fossils is the strongest evidence that there is something very suspicious about the all-pervading "apelike-creature-to-man" evolution story.

SKEPTIC'S CORNER

Skeptics naturally interpret variations of humans and apes as a link between the two. Ever since Darwin proposed that all of life has ascended from a common ancestry, paleoanthropologists have been looking for the elusive "missing link" between man and some sort of ape-like creature. In spite of much publicity to the contrary, this missing link is still missing. The obvious explanation (that this link simply doesn't exist) is ignored because anyone acknowledging this truth would cease to be an evolutionist, and would immediately be ostracized by the modern scientific establishment.

1. *The Bones of Contention: A Creationist Assessment of Human Fossils*, Marvin Lubenow, Baker Books, 2004.

Fabulous Flight

We are taught that some sort of dinosaur, reptile, or amphibian turned into the original bird about 150 million years ago. In other words, over many millions of years a creature with scales, solid bones, muscles meant for crawling motions, and lungs built to absorb air via "in and out breathing" changed into an animal with intricately designed feathers, reinforced hollow bones, muscles designed for a completely new range of motion, and a totally redesigned respiratory system. This happened without leaving a clue in the fossil record as to how this miraculous transformation took place. Let's take our clueless little dinosaur and see how we can transform him into the first bird.

First we zap the mama dinosaur with cosmic rays so her offspring are born with bird muscles instead of dino muscles. Birds have incredibly strong, specialized muscles needed to pull the bird's feather-covered wings downward through air at high speed.

- Unfortunately, the first poor little dinosaur baby has muscles which are in-between flying and walking muscles and quickly becomes a tasty morsel for the first predator who happens along.

- The next baby is born with feathers instead of scales. Not only do the feathers get in the way of movement, but he stands out like a McDonald's sign flashing, "Eat me, eat me." He, too, rapidly becomes a dino burger.

- Our third dino baby is born with the hollow bones needed to keep his weight low enough to enable flight. But alas, he doesn't have the rest of the equipment needed for flight and breaks most of his bones before reaching puberty. Hindered by splints and casts he can't outrun the predators who are now hanging around Mrs. Dino's door to see what other meals are available.

- Baby number four rapidly runs out of breath when trying to escape the predators lined up for an easy meal. His partially transformed lungs just don't work right as either dinosaur or bird.

- Baby number five didn't get any of the characteristics of a bird but happened to be born thinking he was a bird with all the instincts of a bird. As soon as he got out of Mama's nest, he decided to take a flying leap off the nearest cliff while flapping his front legs in a valiant imitation of flight. His carcass immediately became the next meal for nearby scavengers.

Birds are designed to be birds. Their hollow bones are a reinforced engineering wonder having internal trusses designed to give maximum strength with minimum weight. No reptile has anything close to this hollow bone design.

Birds have three distinct types of feathers - primary feathers, which are asymmetric in appearance; secondary, which are slightly asymmetric; and tertiary, which are symmetric on each side of the quill. All three are specifically designed and placed on the bird in order to facilitate flight. All of these feathers have a center stem on which the parts we often think of as being feathers are attached. On one edge of each barb are hooks (barbicels), and on the adjacent barb are slightly convex matching latches (barbules). This attachment forms a sliding joint allowing the feather to bend and flex yet resist air flow through the feather. Since this attachment is a sliding joint, it requires lubrication supplied by oil from a gland which the bird spreads over the feathers with its beak. This gland is also absent from any supposed reptilian "bird ancestor". Birds have muscles which move over a "pulley mechanism" in order to pull the wing downward in a power stroke. Without this muscle, no flight would be possible. No dinosaur, reptile, or amphibian has ever been found with such a muscle/bone arrangement - only birds.

Birds expend enormous amounts of energy to fly. Thus they are constantly foraging for food. The massive energy requirement of their bodies in flight requires a higher oxygen intake rate than reptiles or amphibians. Thus the air

SKEPTIC'S CORNER

Would evolution textbooks and museum displays still be featuring archaeopteryx if anything better had been found? This crown prince of evolutionary fossils already has fully formed feathers, hollow bones, redesigned muscles, and an avian respiratory system. It is obviously just an extinct bird variety not significantly different from many living birds. Displaying the fossilized bones of some land-dwelling reptile beside the bones of a modern bird with a similar skeletal structure does nothing to show how the specialized features of birds could have formed, nor does it prove that some sort of reptile turned into a bird.

sacs in avian lungs have a counter-flow arrangement such that oxygen and carbon dioxide are simultaneously filling and discharging, rather than acting in distinct breaths (taking in oxygen followed by expelling CO_2). It is totally unknown how to transform a reptilian lung into a bird lung in some step-by-step process. Any intermediate lung is total fantasy.

These are just a few of the totally unanswered problems with the whimsical story that some sort of creature turned into a bird. There are many more problems as we look at specialized features which allow birds to hover in the air, migrate 12,000 miles from Pole to Pole, fly backwards and upside down, or perform a laundry list of other marvelous acrobatics. Yet an evolutionist's faith must be extended even further as he attempts to explain the wonder of evolving flight three more times - in insects, bats, and extinct flying reptiles - always with little or no concrete evidence from the fossil record.

Busy Bees

Imagine that you find yourself in a foreign country with no clue how to communicate in the native language. Because communication is difficult you take long hikes and one day discover a treasure trove ten miles outside of town. Immediately, you go to the town surveyor's office to stake claim to the piece of abandoned property upon which the treasure rests. Because you do not know the language, you perform a dance to show the direction and distance to the treasure. In front of the surveyor you waggle your body from side to side while turning in "figure 8" circles. Each complete "figure 8" represents one mile and the angle of your primary "figure 8" movement shows the direction to the treasure relative to the sun.

Not only do you fail to receive the deed to the desired plot of land, you are immediately thrown into the local insane asylum! Yet bees perform just such a feat in hives around the world.

Bees are the only insects which produce large quantities of food eaten by man. A hive of more than 40,000 honey bees must visit over two million flowers to produce a pound of honey, and a single bee visits an average of a thousand flowers a day - providing a critical transfer of pollen between flowers, resulting in seed formation. To produce a pound of honey, the bees in a single hive travel the equivalent of two to three times around the entire globe. The distinctive buzzing sound of the bee comes from the incredible 11,000 wing strokes per minute needed to hoist its heavy body into the air. But one of the bee's most amazing feats is its method of communicating with other bees.

Whenever a single honey bee finds a large source of nectar, it returns to the hive and performs a very specific dance to let the others know where to find the new field of flowering plants. Bees dance in "figure 8" circles and wiggle their bodies in a very specific way to represent the distance and direction to the food source (relative to the sun). The language of the dance is so distinctive that both bees and researchers watching dancing bees can immediately move out from a hive and find the same source of flowering plants.

How do bees hatch with both the ability to perform this dance and the ability to understand its meaning? How do their little bee brains allow them to find their way back to their hives after flying in what seems like aimless circles for miles? How do they know what to do with the nectar and how much honey is needed to survive the winter? And how did the interrelationship between bees and flowers come about?

It is commonly taught in public schools that bees evolved thirty to forty million years ago, whereas flowering plants go back 130 to 160 million years ago.

is the subject of heated debate.) According to evolutionary theory, flowers (which need bees for proper pollination) and bees (which need flowers for food) somehow evolved independently and then just found each other. Yet it has never been explained how a flower that needs bees and bees that need flowers developed by chance mutational changes in some "pre-flower" bee or some "pre-bee" plant [flower]. What did these pre-flower bees and pre-bee plants [flowers] look like? No one knows. How could both organisms develop independently when they need each other to thrive? No one really knows. Why is this development missing in the fossil record? How did a single honey bee develop, when bees must live in a colony, which includes a queen who can lay fertile eggs, workers who feed her and specialize in their labor, and drones whose only function is to mate?

Even more amazing is the design of certain plants which contain "an inexhaustible number of contrivances [to ensure their pollination].[1] For instance, the bucket orchard flower has a slippery lip, causing a bee to fall into a bucket of liquid which is designed to allow exit through a narrow tunnel via the aid of steps within the interior of the flower. Pollen sacs are placed so that they glue onto the bee's back as it exits. The next flower visited has a mechanism to remove the pollen from the bee's back to complete pollination. The entire design, including the bucket, slippery surface, exit tunnel, and pollen attachment/detachment mechanism, are specifically designed for the size, shape, and ability of bees. Surely the belief that bees are the result of blind mutational change is the only blindness actually involved.

1. *The Origin of the Species*, Charles Darwin, Mentor, New York, republished in 1958, p.179.

Incest and Adam

"If Adam and Eve were really the first people and they only had three sons - Cain, Abel, and Seth - where did the rest of us come from?"   This is one of the most common questions used to ridicule the authenticity of the Bible as a historical document. The answer to this conundrum actually provides one of the strongest evidences that the human race was very recently created and has not descended from some sort of ape-like creature over millions of years.

Genesis 5:4 makes the simple yet profound statement that "[Adam & Eve] had sons and daughters." Thus the second generation of humanity had to have been the result of the marriage of brothers and sisters. This concept is completely foreign today, but the commonness of such unions in the distant past is an important clue supporting the recent creation of humanity. For instance, Abraham was married to his half-sister; Abraham's brother Nahor married his brother's daughter; Lot had sexual relations with both of his daughters (which resulted in two Middle Eastern people groups); Isaiah married his second cousin (his dad's brother's granddaughter); Babylonian and Egyptian royalty routinely married brothers and sisters. All of these unions occurred more than three thousand years ago.

Today there are laws to keep brothers, sisters, and cousins from marrying. The reason for this is that the human genome now contains so many mistakes (i.e. genetic mutations) that if two close relatives marry, the resulting children are almost assured to have birth defects or some other physical and/or mental disorder.

With every generation, permanent mistakes build up on the finely tuned information system we call the human DNA genome. These mistakes also contribute to the aging process, as rapidly reproducing cells (such as skin and muscle tissue) sag and deteriorate with increasing numbers of "copying errors." Today, it is rare for five generations to be alive at once, as compared to the original humans who lived well over five hundred years and were likely to have several dozen generations all alive and intermarrying at the same time. In contrast, current human life spans average a mere eighty years. Pictured are four generations of the Toles/Miner/Schlosser/Podboy family line. It is sadly obvious how quickly our bodies deteriorate today - especially compared to Adam and Eve who lived over 900 years due to their DNA having far less degraded information than our DNA today.

Our DNA is actually an enormous encyclopedia of information. Imagine randomly changing hundreds of letters in an encyclopedia before printing and repeating this process for each subsequent printing. Occasionally, new words might be created from the random changes. However, these new random words would not be ordered intelligently and therefore would constitute both a loss of information and wrong information. In each subsequent printing, the information in the encyclopedia would become more and more distorted. Even though the encyclopedia contained millions of letters, it would not be long before the information content would become quite garbled. The same is true of the human DNA code … and the speed with which this is happening testifies to how recently the human DNA code had to have been created.

Because we now know each generation of humans accumulates more mistakes on their genome than the previous generation, there must have been fewer mistakes on the genome of people at a time closer to their original creation. This explains why people living only thousands of years ago could have married close relations with no apparent problems, while today this is considered dangerous, immoral, illegal, and incestuous. It was for our own good that God instituted laws against marriage of close relations at the time of Moses (approximately 3,400 years ago), whereas before this time there was no such prohibition. The only unchanging restrictions which God placed upon mankind were for one man to unite with one woman in a permanent life-long bond of marriage. This has not changed, and whenever this ideal pattern is ignored (via infidelity, promiscuity, polygamy, or homosexuality) interpersonal relationship disasters result. This was true in early biblical history, and it is still true today.

It is the speed with which the human genome has deteriorated that testifies to our recent creation. The downward deterioration of the human DNA code is obvious. How could mutations improve the brain size, stature, intelligence, tool-using ability, communication ability, longevity, and a host of other features of some sort of ape-like creature over the million supposed years leading up to mankind's appearance, when over the last 4,500 years of recorded history it is obvious that these same mutations are driving humanity's DNA code downward? This rapid change fits the historical evidence if humanity was created a mere 6,000 years ago, but this rapid deterioration makes no sense if humanity is in excess of a million years old.

Evolutionists label the complex gecko foot as an example of "adaptive evolution," and fossil finds such as the gecko foot encapsulated in amber are considered chance occurrences. Yet what is "adaptive evolution"? How could the DNA code of a "pre-gecko lizard" have randomly mutated to form the very specific structure needed to suction themselves to surfaces? How could the specific muscular movements needed to stick and release these millions of pads have developed simultaneously? This requires detailed and specific information added to the DNA code. Where is the fossil evidence showing how all this developed? How could a gecko foot have been caught in "slowly oozing sap?" Why wouldn't the foot have decayed long before becoming encapsulated, unless rapidly buried in a massive flood event? Labeling the gecko foot an "adaptive evolution" development explains nothing and relies on hand-waving and hubris to deny an obviously, intelligently designed creation.

38

"Evolution is a fact." This is the mental filter through which naturalists evaluate all fossil finds and scientific data. Therefore, no matter what is found in the fossil record, biological world, or throughout the universe, the data is forced to fit the model of evolution. The gecko is an example of this.

This complex lizard is capable of walking on surfaces as slippery as glass and leaping from vertical surface to vertical surface - sticking like glue upon landing. Biologists have debated for decades what mechanism allows this common creature to defy gravity by running upside down across ceilings. The oldest known gecko fossil prior to 2008 (essentially identical to modern geckos) was found in rock layers dated by evolutionary assumptions at 50 million years. It was therefore believed that prior to 50 million years ago some simpler form of lizard had slowly evolved the ability to cling to walls and ceilings.

In late 2008 a gecko foot (essentially identical to a modern gecko foot) was found encapsulated in amber and discovered in rock layers assumed to be 100 million years old. Thus 50 million years of evolutionary advancement simply disappeared, and the supposed development of the complex gecko foot was pushed earlier. The fact that each gecko find is essentially a modern gecko and that nothing has been found leading up to the unique gecko foot does nothing to shake the dogmatic belief in evolution; new finds simply are absorbed and time frames shifted.[1]

The foot of the gecko is anything but simple. The gecko is designed with toe pads tipped with tiny fibers, each of which is tipped with a suction-cup-like flattened surface only 0.000008 inch in diameter. If each tiny suction pad were the size of a dime, the gecko's foot would be one mile across and contain more pads than the number of people living in the United States. But this would be useless without a mechanism for compressing and releasing the estimated 500 million suction pads on the lizard's toes. Using a scanning electron microscope to magnify the gecko toes 35,000 times, scientists discovered that gecko feet are designed to slide and peel the suction pads loose with each step so that the lizard can rapidly move across a vertical or inverted surface. No other animal exhibits this unique design, and there is no evidence of any "in-between" transitional gecko foot on any animal – alive or fossilized.

Biblical creation is based upon the relatively recent creation of very different creatures, with a wide variety of abilities, by an infinitely powerful, unbelievably creative God. The originally created gecko "kind" would have had an enormous DNA variability, making it capable of producing a wide variety of geckos, such that varying geckos could fill different environmental niches. (There are 2,000 known species of geckos alive today.) Yet the basic gecko "kind" would not vary beyond established genetic limits. Furthermore, in the creation model of earth history, there was an energetic flood which ripped up all vegetation upon the planet and re-deposited it within sediment layers, forming coal, rock, and fossil seams around the world. If this model were true, you would expect to find complex creatures such as geckos in the fossil record with the same functional features as geckos alive today (such as the gecko foot), but no transitional forms of very complex features. This biblical model is exactly what observations such as the recently discovered amber-encased gecko foot confirm.

The recently discovered amber-encapsulated gecko foot, supposedly 100 million years old, was identical in every way to modern gecko feet, showing no change in the foot over all this supposed vast passage of time. This agrees perfectly with what would be expected from the creation model. The very fact that enormous amounts of amber exist also fits the creation/flood model. As sap-containing trees (such as pines) were crushed during the flood, sap would have been forced out rapidly to form the extensive amber deposits (which are mined for jewelry in the Baltic Sea region). Many small creatures and insects became trapped within the thickening sap, only to be rapidly buried and crystallized before decay could occur. No such mechanism is happening today. The appearance of the gecko foot (identical to modern gecko feet) within amber deposits (the extensive burial of which testifies to a massive catastrophe) is explained well by the creation model of earth history.

1. *Fossilized Gecko Fits Creation Model*, Brian Thomas, www.answersingenesis.org, 9/8/2008.

The Heart of the Matter

As the great physicist finished his almost incomprehensible lecture on the reality of time, space, matter, and the mathematical principles which rule the forces of nature, a stunned and reverent silence fell over the crowd. Who would dare challenge his vast knowledge with additional questions? Perhaps because he had no reputation to lose, perhaps because his mind worked in simple terms, one struggling undergraduate timidly raised his hand to ask, "Could you explain again where the matter and energy came from to start the universe?" The answer was given in technical terms even more incomprehensible and with less clarity than before. The perplexed student dared to ask a follow-up question, "But what was the origin of all the complex stuff we find in the universe?" Again the answer was a non-answer. It was as if the great man had been asked the sum of one plus one and could not respond. Yet it was the undergraduate student who dared to ask the obvious…rather than the renowned physicist, stumped by a simple question…who was ushered out of the hall amidst insults and anger.

In a similar fashion to this story, simple questions about the origin of organs remain largely unanswered, and it is those who dare to question natural explanations who are vilified. Just how did the complex organs of life develop? Blood is central to life, and a pumping heart is required in all higher animals to circulate the blood. But few stop to ask the obvious, "How could a creature such as a jellyfish, which functions perfectly well without a heart, have developed such a complex organ?"

The human heart is the most amazing pump ever devised. It develops enough pumping pressure to shoot blood twenty feet through the air, and each day it pumps 2,000 gallons of life-giving blood through enough blood vessels contained within a single human to circle the entire earth four times. Over the course of a typical human life, this tiny twelve-ounce organ beats approximately three billion times and pumps sixty million gallons of blood through our bodies. The heart has an intricate system of nerves to detect problems and the entire system is capable of reproducing exact copies of its muscle tissue by cell division. No pump built by man comes close to performing a similar set of functions and is capable of operating essentially maintenance-free for over a hundred years.

No one finding a hand-stroked balloon pump, a foot-operated bicycle pump, a small electric aquarium pump, an automobile fuel pump, and a huge city water supply pump all buried in a field would believe that one had randomly turned into the other. No one would believe that any of these pumps just developed by a random arrangement of parts. Yet evolutionists line up the simple heart of an earthworm, the two-chambered heart of a fish, the three-chambered heart of an amphibian, and the four-chambered heart of a mammal as an explanation for where the human heart came from. Educators would have us accept that random changes guided by natural selection are the only possible explanation for the human heart.

Each of us is only one heartbeat away from finding the true answer to the origin of our heart. The problem is, once that last beat happens, it is too late to act upon the truth we will find. Fortunately, there is already plenty of evidence that our hearts exist because we have a Creator.

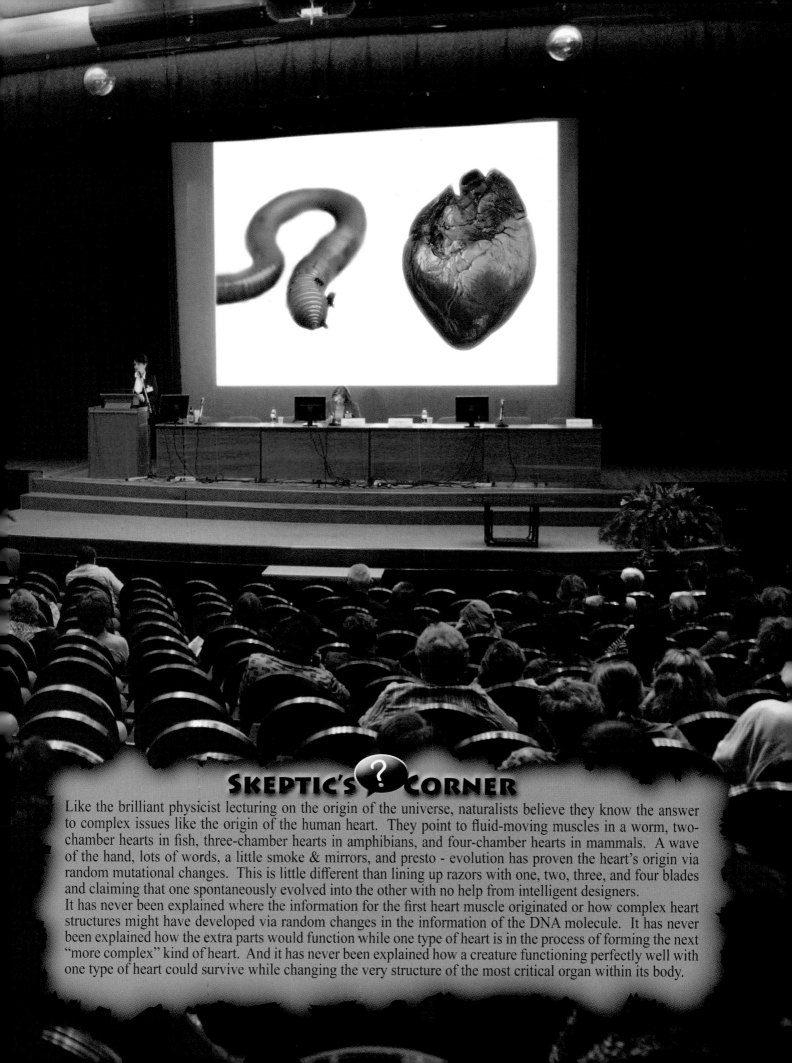

SKEPTIC'S CORNER

Like the brilliant physicist lecturing on the origin of the universe, naturalists believe they know the answer to complex issues like the origin of the human heart. They point to fluid-moving muscles in a worm, two-chamber hearts in fish, three-chamber hearts in amphibians, and four-chamber hearts in mammals. A wave of the hand, lots of words, a little smoke & mirrors, and presto - evolution has proven the heart's origin via random mutational changes. This is little different than lining up razors with one, two, three, and four blades and claiming that one spontaneously evolved into the other with no help from intelligent designers.

It has never been explained where the information for the first heart muscle originated or how complex heart structures might have developed via random changes in the information of the DNA molecule. It has never been explained how the extra parts would function while one type of heart is in the process of forming the next "more complex" kind of heart. And it has never been explained how a creature functioning perfectly well with one type of heart could survive while changing the very structure of the most critical organ within its body.

The Simple Cell Hoax

Ernst Haeckel was an atheist who studied the "grandeur of a Godless nature" and was absolutely convinced that molecules-to-man evolution was a fact. A gifted speaker, he devoted his life to popularizing this idea through books and working-class lectures in rented halls. His talks were media extravaganzas of the day, as he covered the front of the music halls with immense fossil displays, massive charts, and plentiful pictures. In 1868, only nine years after reading Darwin's landmark volume on how all life was related, the German scientist and master showman proposed a link between non-living matter and the "simple living cell."

Nothing had been found linking inanimate chemicals to living cells, so Dr. Haeckel invented a series of minute organisms which he called "Monera" and promoted pictures of these shapeless blobs of protoplasm (without nuclei) in his books and lectures. Haeckel authoritatively proposed that these pre-cell creatures reproduced by a process that he called "fission." Later the same year Thomas Huxley, another talented orator and atheist from England, reported finding such microscopic organisms in deep-sea mud samples. They were dubbed "*Bathybius haeckelii,*" in honor of Haeckel and were promoted through universities and popular media as proof of evolution. Despite the fact that these organisms were shown to be a mistake in 1875 they continued to be promoted as proof of evolution for the next 50 years by Haeckel's uncorrected and widely circulated book, ***History of Creation.***

It turned out that biological samples were routinely preserved in alcohol, and a chemist more committed to truth than evolution demonstrated that sea water blended with alcohol results in precipitated sulphate of lime (gypsum) which looked like a small gelatinous cell without a nucleus. These little "cells" became trapped in bits of exoskeleton of plankton and had been misinterpreted as a precursor to life called *Bathybius haeckelii.* The report showing that this was all a mistake was buried in an obscure journal and essentially ignored because the implications were too damaging to those promoting the evolutionary viewpoint to the general public.[1]

In almost 200 years of searching, scientists have never found an explanation for how a living cell could arise from non-living matter. Darwin and his contemporaries thought of the cell as a rather simple structure upon which more complex life could develop. In actuality, any living cell is a machine so complicated that there is no comparable human-manufactured counterpart capable of reproducing exact replicas of itself. The cell is simply far too complex to ever have developed by any natural process.

The tiniest single cell bacterium is made from the specific arrangement of 100 billion atoms and is as complex as a city. It has a central memory bank, assembly/processing units, and packing/shipping centers. It has an elaborate communication system with quality control procedures and repair mechanisms and can produce its own army to attack invaders. Its protective wall allows waste products out while preventing unwanted substances from entering. The cell is filled with thousands of "robot-like" machines designed to perform specific functions due to their three-dimensional structure. There is a master library, power plants, and trash disposal centers. If the DNA in a single bacterial cell were the thickness of fishing line, it would be 125 miles long and coiled inside a

SKEPTIC'S CORNER

A headline from September, 2008 is typical of chemicals-to-life research discoveries: "*Biologists on the Verge of Creating New Form of Life.*" Note the text of the article:

"A team of biologists and chemists is closing in on bringing non-living matter to life. A lab led by Jack Szostak, molecular biologist at Harvard Medical School, is building simple cell models that can almost be called life. Szostak's protocells are built from fatty molecules that can trap bits of nucleic acids that contain the source code for replication. Combined with a process that harnesses external energy from the sun or chemical reactions, they could form a self-replicating, evolving system that satisfies the conditions of life. It isn't anything like life on earth now, but might represent life as it began or could exist elsewhere in the universe ..."[3]

Notice the language "can **almost** be called life...**could trap**...**combined with** [other abilities which have unknown natural origins]...**could form**... **might represent**". Even more revealing is the fact that the nature of this "discovery" is not unique. Basically, fatty molecules circled around bits of DNA which were placed in a test tube. Common dish soap would behave similarly. Soap molecules would likewise surround DNA fragments and turn one end toward the water. The fact that "fatty molecules" do the same is hardly a major revelation. Promoting finds which are this insignificant reveals that natural explanations for life have advanced little since the *Bathybius haeckelii* fiasco.

structure the size of a basketball. The entire string can be unwound and copied at three times the speed of a spinning airplane propeller without tangling the line and with very rare mistakes.[2]

The incredible complexity of any living cell, with its hundreds of thousands of interdependent parts, screams "creation." The fact that no experiment has come remotely close to showing how chemicals could come alive - in spite of millions of hours and billions of dollars spent - is one of the strongest testimonies that we do, indeed, have a Creator. The fact that textbooks still present the development of the cell as a product of some natural process is as irresponsible as leaving *Bathybius haeckelii* in **History of Creation** in subsequent editions for 50 years after it was clearly shown to be a blatant mistake.

1. *In the Minds of Men*, Ian Taylor, TFE publications, p. 180-185, 2003.
2. *Evolution: A Theory in Crisis*, Michael Denton, Adler & Adler, 1985.
3. www.wired.com/wiredscience/2008/09/biologists-on-t/comment-page-15/.

SKEPTIC'S CORNER

Evolutionists line up plants into evolutionary sequences not because of the overwhelming evidence from either living organisms or the fossil record but because of a devotion to the presupposition of naturalism. A recent example of evolutionary storytelling is the "discovery" that a plant called teosinte is the direct ancestor of modern corn. It is reported that this plant (which looks very different from modern corn) has chromosomes indistinguishable from commercial corn. In addition, an analysis using repetitive DNA elements found in most genomes identified teosinte as the "immediate ancestor of corn" and a cross between corn and teosinte yields healthy, fertile offspring. Yet what has really been discovered is just an ancestral variation of modern corn. This fits perfectly into the biblical understanding that an infinitely creative Designer put a wide variety of information into the genetic code of the different types of plants and animals which He originally created.

It would seem that no matter what the evidence, it is forced to fit the dogma of evolution. If no fossil transitions are found, it is because creatures evolved too rapidly to leave any evidence (punctuated equilibrium); yet when wide variations within a species are found, it is spun as evidence of evolution in action. Everything, useful or not, functional or not, beneficial or detrimental, is spun as evidence for evolution.

If the gulf between man and apes is a leap between skyscrapers, the chasm between each of the twenty-nine classes of plants is like the abyss separating the rims of the Grand Canyon. According to evolutionary theory, each of these very distinct twenty-nine groupings of plants came from some previous plant via random mutational changes. Yet plant fossils clearly fall into the same twenty-nine classes. Nothing has ever been found to bridge the gap between any of the distinctly different types of plants, nor is it understood how one could slowly modify, say a fern, to turn it into a pine tree (the closest fern-type "relative" listed on typical relationship charts). Furthermore, every transitional intermediate form between the fern and the pine tree would need to be functional and advantageous or it would not survive.

Evolutionary texts on plant evolution commonly use terms such as "probably," "may have," "apparently," "presumably," etc. Yet honest acknowledgements such as this statement by Dr. Tom Kemp, Curator of Zoological Collections at Oxford University, are rare, *"In virtually all cases a new taxon [type of plant] appears for the first time in the fossil record with most definitive features already present [identical to modern plants], and practically no known stem-group forms [no transitional forms]."* **Fossils and Evolution**, Oxford University Press, 1999. [note: bracketed clarifications mine]

Plants are divided into two main groups, the Bryata (which do not have the "plumbing" features needed for transporting water) and the Tracheata (which do). Obviously, the water-transporting-type plants are more complex (having additional features), so they should be buried higher up in the fossil record (having evolved later). Yet the opposite is true. Plants from the Tracheata group (such as ferns) are found at lower fossil levels than those from the Bryata group (such as moss).[1] From the very start the evolutionary story of plant evolution involves explaining away the actual evidence.

Bacteria supposedly turned into blue-green algae; yet bacteria and algae are as different as bicycles and motorcycles. It is possible to line up a bicycle, a motorcycle, and an automobile and authoritatively state, "See the evolution of transportation," but what does this prove? All three were designed by intelligent creators and the automobile actually preceded the motorcycle in developmental sequence. In a similar way, the lining up of plants or creatures via design similarity does not prove that one turned into another by natural processes.

Next on the evolutionary lineup, algae apparently turned into plankton, seaweed, and other vastly different plant forms. Once again the evolutionary origin of each is pure storytelling as no intermediates exist. From here the story gets complicated and fuzzier. Following one branch, green algae turned into whisk ferns, that turned into "real" ferns, that turned into pine-type tree - that also branched out into the "superstars of diversity and abundance" - the million known species of flowering plants - each of which may have numerous varieties. For instance, corn, rice, and grapes are all capable of enormous variability with entire research centers collecting and cross-breeding varieties with up to a million different known variations of each. Yet corn remains corn, rice remains rice, and grapes remain grapes - both in modern laboratories and in the fossil record.[2]

Plants are incredibly complex and specialized organisms. Ferns morphing into non-ferns is simply fantasy. Yet the only viable alternative is that God created different kinds of plants to reproduce after their own "kind" (with enormous variability within that kind). The evidence, both from the laboratory and the fossil record, clearly supports the creation alternative.

1. *Kingdom of the Plants: Defying Evolution*, Alexander Williams, Creation 24(1);46-48, 2001.
2. *Evolution Exposed*, Roger Patterson, Answers in Genesis Publications, 2006.

A Horse is a Horse

In the early 1800's, Europe had a strongly Christian culture. Very few doubted the existence of a Creator or questioned the Bible as an authoritative source of truth. Today Europe is essentially an atheistic culture, where the Bible is considered irrelevant. How did the enemies of Christianity transform this culture?

First to fall was the timeline of the Bible, as Charles Lyell, a lawyer-turned-geologist, proposed slow and gradual processes over eons of time as an alternative to the worldwide flood. This idea replaced the acknowledgement of a global flood as the explanation for the geological features of our planet. Following close on his heels was Charles Darwin, proposing that all of biology could be explained by slow gradual changes over eons of time as an explanation for the biological diversity of our planet. This direct attack on the authority of God's Word did not achieve immediate acceptance because it failed to explain the development of highly complex organisms. Nor did it really explain how enormously complicated and interdependent organs such as the eyeball could have developed gradually. To sway the masses, evolution proponents needed a visual, easily understood example of "evolution in action" which could be grasped by both the highly educated student and the man on the street. They needed an icon around which to rally. They found their publicity gold mine in the horse.

Up until the early 1900's, horses were THE mode of transportation used by individuals and industry alike. Everyone was familiar with the common horse. In 1876, T.H. Huxley, "Darwin's Bulldog," visited an arrangement of horse fossils collected and arranged by Yale University paleontologist Othniel Marsh. Huxley immediately recognized the potential of this sequence for popularizing evolution. Here at last was an icon of evolution with which everyone could connect - a sequence of creatures showing a small, four-toed, "pre-horse" creature with short teeth, changing into a larger, three- toed creature, followed by a two-toed creature, ending in a one-toed (hoofed) horse of much greater size, complete with the modern long teeth.

SKEPTICS ? CORNER

The evolution of the horse icon is so well known that evolutionists cannot simply discard it, regardless of the disarray which the fossil record reveals. Therefore, the supposed sequence continues to be displayed in museums and textbooks even though there is significant overlapping of the various forms of horses throughout the geological layers. These overlaps are simply censored and ignored so that the sequence can be maintained.

This was "evolution in action," dug right out of the rock record, mounted and displayed for all to see. The famous horse sequence soon filled textbooks and museums around the world. Imagine the impact on the belief and thought processes of a generation who were totally dependent upon horses for their very economic survival.

It is only now, over a hundred years after the damage has been done, that evolutionists sheepishly admit that the horse sequence was largely fantasy.[1] For instance, Dr. Niles Eldredge, former curator of the American Museum of Natural History, has stated, *"There have been an awful lot of stories, some more imaginative than others, about what the nature of that history [of life] really is. The most famous example, still on exhibit downstairs [in the American Museum] is the exhibit on horse evolution prepared perhaps 50 years ago. Now I think that is lamentable, particularly when the people who proposed those kind of stories may themselves be aware of the speculative nature of some of that stuff."[2]*

There is no undisputed sequence of creatures leading from some small, furry animal to the modern horse. The smallest ancestors to the modern horse have been found in the same rock layers as essentially modern horses. Fully grown modern horses vary in size from the less than two-foot-tall Fallabella to the over six-foot-tall Clydesdale. Claiming that different varieties of co-existing horse-like creatures are ancestors to each other is analogous to claiming that one fifty-year-old man is the great, great, great, great, great grandfather of another fifty-year-old-man who lives in the same house.

What the fossil record of horses actually reveals is not an evolutionary sequence with some small ancestor of the horse slowly turning into the modern horse but lots of different types of horses with an enormous amount of variation within a given, originally created, horse "kind." This variation may very well include different hoof types, including different numbers of toes, body sizes, tooth shapes, and skull structure. But these are just varieties which came forth from the enormous information content of the original coded DNA. This allowed different creatures to adapt and survive in different environments. Many did not adapt well after the worldwide flood and are no longer around to study except as fossils in the rock layers.

It is the saddest of ironies that one of the most pervasive icons of evolution (the horse series), which has been used for over a century to destroy people's belief in biblical truth, is based on evidence which actually fits better into a straightforward understanding of the Bible. It would seem that a horse really is a horse, of course.

1. *In the Minds of Men*, p. 147, Ian Taylor, TFE Publishing, 2008.

2. Niles Eldredge, quoted in *Darwin's Enigma*, p.78, Luther Sutherland

We have all heard that the belief in God is a "leap of faith". Yet the Bible, from the Old Testament (Psalms 19:1-4) to the New Testament (Romans 1:18-23), clearly states that the reality of God's existence is absolutely apparent to everyone, everywhere - simply by observing creation. In other words, it is merely by observing nature that everyone will realize that a Creator made it. Yet if any part of "bacteria-to-Bob" type of evolutionary transformation is true, then there is no evidence for God's existence by observing nature.

I sometimes think that God created many things just to see our jaw-dropping, awe-struck, I-can't–believe-it reaction; that same kind of wonder expressed by a small child who first discovers the softness of a puppy or the fragile beauty of a butterfly. The lowly leafhopper displays just such a feature.

The September 13, 2013 journal Science described a set of perfectly formed gears at the base of the 1/16" long leafhopper nymph. This creature has the ability to jump several inches using a mighty thrust from its hind legs that propels the creature with an acceleration of nearly 400 g (fighter pilots risk blackout if accelerating much past 10 g). This feat would be equivalent to a man accelerating from 0 to 2000 mph in 0.002 seconds and jumping 400 feet in a single bound!

What makes the leafhoppers feat even more amazing is that the nerve impulses cannot travel fast enough to allow both legs to push off in a coordinated fashion – meaning that with every hop the insect should spin out of control. So how did the Creator solve this problem? He added a set of interlocking gears to the base of the leafhopper's legs so that they had to fire in exact coordination.[1] This design is currently being studied as a prototype for a new kind of high speed directional gear.

The marvels and wonders of God's creativity, as revealed through the microscope never cease to amaze. The belief that such a gear could "make itself" via random changes over time is equivalent to believing that a gear could be produced in a machine shop via random hammering of a piece of metal. The real leap of faith is the belief in evolution, not the belief in a designer God.

1. *Answers Magazine*, Vol. 9 No. 1, Jar. 2014, p.13.

SKEPTIC'S ? CORNER

There are only two possibilities for the intricate gear mechanism found in the leafhopper. Either: 1) they were simply created, intact and fully formed by a Creator, or 2) something slowly evolved into the intricate gears. Evolution ASSUMES that somehow small changes happened to the DNA of some previous insect-like creature, each change along the way having some useful purpose or was for some reason kept, and somehow the gears formed themselves. There is not a shred of evidence supporting the fanciful belief that the gears of the leafhopper made themselves.

Gaggles of Geese

Last spring my wife observed a pair of Canada geese swimming along with six newly hatched goslings. Suddenly a dog ran at them and the goslings dove under the water, scattering in all different directions and popping up moments later in different parts of the pond. Meanwhile, the parents swam directly at the dog and started flapping their wings and hissing ominously. The comical escapade raised numerous questions: How did the baby geese know to scatter in different directions rather than stay together? Why would the adults put themselves at risk in order to protect their young? If the first foolish goose to try this was killed, how did its young survive? How does knowledge learned in one generation get transferred as a born instinct?

Canada geese migrate up to 3,000 miles each fall, returning in the spring to essentially the same nesting grounds where they had originally hatched. How do they know how to do this? Even if their young learn this skill from their parents, how did the first goose know it was warmer in the south? Who taught geese to fly in a "V" pattern, which provides trailing birds with a significant lift advantage? Why do geese fall out of formation and stay with an injured goose instead of flying on with the rest of the flock? How do they know how to navigate through unknown territory to reach their desired destination? Why do they mate for life when more offspring could be produced if they mated indiscriminately? In summary, where do instincts come from?

Creation acknowledges that these advanced skills, which seem to be implanted in an animal's consciousness, were placed there by the same entity which formed the physical structure of the animal's body. Thus instincts perfectly match an animal's needs and abilities. The reason animals are born with these skills and parents are born with the ability to teach their offspring the necessary survival skills is because these instincts are pre-programmed at birth.

A common example given for instinct development is imprinting. Baby geese will follow around the first creature they encounter after hatching, thereby imprinting this creature into their mind as their "mother." Naturalists suggest that a similar process could imprint instincts upon a newly hatched creature. Yet even this characteristic is already pre-programmed into the geese. From where did the ability come in the first place? There is no adequate answer, other than creation.

The idea of an instinct developing by random chance processes is simply "too costly" to the evolving organism. Suppose some pre-bird creature decided it should fly. Even if it miraculously had all the proper equipment (hollow bones, rapid metabolism, feathers, restructured muscles, etc.) from where did the instinct telling it how to use all its new equipment come? Bird after bird would die while trying to develop the new flying ability, and those creatures who were not wasting time and energy in this "instinct development process" would be thriving and taking over the population. Natural selection would actually favor those creatures not trying to develop new instincts.

A good analogy would be a gaggle of geese waddling across a busy interstate highway wearing blindfolds. Even if one goose did manage to make it to the other side, how would it tell a yet-to-be-born gosling how to accomplish this feat? Meanwhile, the massive number of dead geese lying on the road would make such instinct development far too biologically costly.

Evolution has no answer for how instincts develop. Try searching for "instinct evolution" on the internet. Evolutionists essentially claim that creatures with the best instincts survive the best; therefore, they claim, the fact that instincts help animals survive prove that instincts evolved.

The problem for evolution is that learned behavior is not transferred from generation to generation. Try teaching your dog a complex behavior such as shaking hands, rolling over, or bringing you the newspaper from the front porch. Once your dog has pups, give the pups the same command. They'll cock their heads and look at you like you are crazy. Not once in a billion tries will the behavior learned by the parent be instinctively transferred to the offspring. This is scientific reality.

Instincts are critical for life; yet they cannot be explained by any known natural process - including natural selection. On the other hand, the many instincts necessary for the survival of geese is exactly what would be expected if the goose was made by an unfathomably intelligent Creator who wanted many variations of such a creature to survive in a wide variety of habitats.

Monkey See, Monkey Do

It took New Tribe missionaries over two years to learn enough of the Mouk language to communicate effectively. The Mouk people had lived in a secluded river village for thousands of years and the village was several days' travel via canoe from the nearest town in Papua, New Guinea. After the missionaries had learned to communicate, they told the natives that many people in the far-away country of America believe that humans came from some sort of monkey (like the nearby caged animal awaiting its destiny as the main course for supper). The natives looked at the monkey in the cage, looked at each other, looked at the monkey again, and then spontaneously burst out laughing and asked (in essence), "Are your people blind?"[1]

Contrast that with the typical American college student. He has been told hundreds of times in museums, movies, textbooks, school classrooms, magazines, and popular TV shows that mankind's DNA is ninety-seven to ninety-nine percent identical to that of apes. After years of such indoctrination, the typical student readily accepts the idea that this similarity proves that some sort of ape-like creature is our "grandparent." The implied scientific accuracy of mankind being 98.5 percent identical to apes is simply accepted. Yet the chimpanzee DNA code was not even mapped until 2005 and is still incomplete. If neither had been mapped prior to that time, how could we know they were 98.5 percent similar back in the 1970's, when this claim became popularized?

It turns out that the source of this claim was the selection and comparison of only a very small portion of the genetic code of mankind and chimps. Areas of greater differences were simply ignored, and the claim of similarity became an accepted dogma of the educational establishment. Since the total gene mapping of both species has been largely completed the similarity has dropped to ninety-four percent, but even this figure ignores "heterochromatic" DNA.

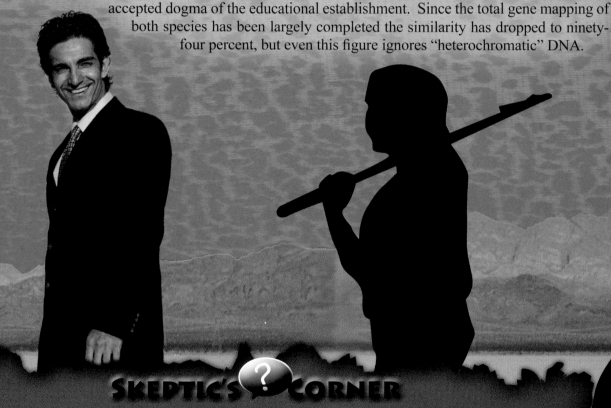

SKEPTIC'S CORNER

There are only two possibilities for our existence: Either we came from some pre-human, ape-like creature which turned into a human, or we were created fully human and fully functional. Either one is true or the other is true, but they can't both be true. Evolution starts by eliminating consideration of the creation option - which leaves only evolution to be presented as a fact. Therefore, when a small part of man's gene sequence is compared to a chimpanzee and similarities are found, the conclusion that one is related to the other is widely promoted. This is why such superficial evidence as gene comparisons are uncritically accepted and widely publicized, to the point that problems with the conclusions are never even exposed to students.

The human DNA genome (library of coded information) is like a string of letters which form sentences, paragraphs, chapters, and books over three billion letters long. When comparing the "human library" and the "chimp library," it turns out that the letters are lined up similarly only about seventy percent of the time with many extra or missing sentences. These extra and missing sentences are essentially ignored when making the comparison between the two codes. There are many physical similarities between chimpanzees and humans because God made both humans and chimps as physical creatures with two arms, legs, eyes, ears, and many other similar structures. Yet we are enormously distinct in many other physical ways, and we are light years apart both mentally and spiritually.

Assuming that some precursor to a chimp turned into both a chimp and a human via random mutational changes filtered by natural selection is like assuming that a bicycle turned into both a Volkswagen Beetle and a Mercedes Benz via random changes at a bicycle factory. God chose to create humans with both a spiritual nature and a physical body. Since the human body has a similar design to other creatures and it must function with a similar biological metabolism, there are obviously going to be enormous similarities in genetic coding.

A mental and physical "Grand Canyon" separates humans from any other creature - including chimpanzees. No creature other than humans and birds walk continuously upright (yet birds are certainly not considered a direct ancestor to mankind). No other mammal controls fire, writes books to pass on knowledge, paints representative art, builds complex machines, or understands abstract concepts such as infinity, zero, or eternity. No other creature prays. The gulf between mankind and animals is not a matter of degree; it is an uncrossed chasm. There are no animals which occasionally understand abstract concepts, sometimes draw portraits, sort of prefer to walk upright, write short novelettes, or pray sporadically. Mankind is enormously unique and the idea that the similarity of human to chimp DNA proves relationship is pure imagination. The Mouk people's laughter at the absurdity of such a belief is a more honest response than the college student's blind acceptance of chimp/human DNA sequencing as evidence of ancestral relationship.

1. "*EE-Taow*", Filmed by New Tribes Missions, 1989.

Orphan Genes Mystify Scientists

The very mention of the word "orphan" brings to mind images of scrawny children begging for bowls of water-thin porridge in dilapidated orphanages. Yet a far more profound meaning has been given to this word in recent years.

The DNA code hidden within every cell of every living organism can be likened to a library of books. This coded information determines the exact body shape, size, and individual characteristics of a creature. Chromosomes are like the books within that library and genes are like specific pages within each book. Every letter on every page is rapidly being acknowledged to have a specific function and purpose.[1] Biologists have also long taught that the closer the letters on each page match, the more closely creatures are related on the evolutionary tree of life. Therefore a family of closely related creatures (such as ants), should have closely related genes which can be traced back to a common ancestor of the specific species being studied. But orphan genes put a fly in the ointment of this belief.

Only ten years ago it took over a decade, millions of dollars, and the partnership of many world renowned genetics laboratories to produce the first complete sequence of the 3 billion letters of the human DNA code. Yet today automated DNA sequences can produce the same code of an individual human for as little as $1500 in a matter of days. We have become so adept at sequencing DNA that the code for over 100 million different sequences are now readily available for comparison. If evolution were actually true, then the sequence of information from one creature as it turned into a slightly modified but similar creature should be like changing a few letters on the page of a book (a specific gene) but easy to determine what original book the modified page came from. Yet the exact opposite is true. The example of ant DNA is a perfect case study representative of practically every other grouping of animals.

Ants are so common that the DNA sequence of a large percentage of the 14,000 known species have now been determined. Yet far from being closely related, the DNA sequence of the specific genes from the 5800 different species in the ant Myrmicinae subfamily have an average of 19% of their gene sequence COMPLETELY and TOTALLY unrelated to any gene sequence found anywhere in the animal kingdom – INCLUDING ANTS IN THEIR OWN SUBSPECIES! This is akin to a printing press producing a closely related sequel to a novel by randomly changing letters on the pages of the original novel so that 20% of the pages are so completely changed that they are TOTALLY unrelated to anything in the original book. Yet the information is completely functional, useful, and understandable in the new novel. These genes are called orphan genes and they fit perfectly with what we would be expected to find in different types of ants designed by a brilliant creator.

SKEPTIC'S ? CORNER

Evolutionists do not have any adequate explanation for why such a huge proportion of very similar creatures have such unique gene sequences. Even the millions-of-years evolutionary timeframe is inadequate to explain how so much information could have COMPLETELY changed from individual pages (gene sequences) of one species of ant to another. In order to promote their belief in a common descent, they chose to emphasize only those genes which show similarity between creatures they assume to be closely "related" - such as the cytochrome C gene of humans and chimpanzees. In this case similarly designed creatures do have a certain gene which are essentially identical, but this is no surprise and hardly a proof of common descent when only a few specific genes are considered. Meanwhile these same scientists ignore vast differences (such as the 30% - or one billion code differences – between man and chimps) for which they have no adequate explanation. This is like saying that trees and kelp are closely related because they both have roots and use photosynthesis while not even trying to explain the origin of the vast differences between the two types of organisms.

A common design would have a large portion of similar coding but additional features, instincts, and abilities would be coded from scratch, not by modifying of existing information. This is exactly what we find.

1. *Biological Information: New Perspectives*, edited by Robert Marks,et.al., *"Not junk after all: non-protein coding DNA carries extensive biological information"*, Jonathan Wells, World Scientific Publishing, 2013.

THE CHICKEN OR THE EGG?

SKEPTIC'S CORNER

For the evolutionist, just the use of the word "evolution" - like the waving of a magic wand by a magician - is sufficient to explain any biological mystery. Because the mechanism to remove information from DNA works so elegantly and is basic to all forms of life, it is simply assumed to have evolved – i.e. made itself. For the mind devoted to naturalism as an explanation for everything, this is sufficient until something better comes along. In reality, evolution relies on faith for the unexplainable, whereas creation relies on the observation that complex, interrelated systems such as information removal from the DNA molecule is best explained by a designer behind all of life.

Some simple questions are unanswerable by modern science because modern science has been defined in such a way that the correct answer is "not allowed". One such question is the simple children's riddle, "Which came first, the chicken or the egg?"

To understand the answer to this riddle, we need to first examine one of the many mysteries of modern biochemistry. Proteins are the most common chemical within our bodies, with an estimated 200,000 different proteins acting as a dizzying variety of microscopic biological machines to perform every manner of transport, construction, disposal, and manipulation of processes within our cells. But where do these very specific little molecular machines come from? It turns out that they are made only from information contained upon the DNA molecules within the nucleus of each cell.

DNA contains a sequential recipe for producing each protein needed within a cell - just like a cookbook recipe for making a soufflé must be followed from the top of the page to the bottom rather than randomly following the directions in any order. But whereas we can obtain the information from the cookbook by merely reading it with our eyes, the mechanism for removing the information from DNA in order to produce a needed protein is enormously more complex.

First, the cell must know that it needs a certain protein (and in what quantity). This involves both measurement and feedback mechanisms. Next, a specially designed protein attaches itself to the DNA molecule in order to open the molecule up at exactly the correct position in order to remove coded

information from the correct location to make the correct protein "recipe". After that, a copying sequence begins such that one letter at a time of information is extracted from the DNA to construct the desired protein molecule while yet another protein attaches itself to the DNA molecule at the correct location to stop the copying process. Finally, another specifically designed protein zips the DNA molecule closed again after the copying process is complete.[1]

Now here's the mystery: no biologically useful proteins can be made until the DNA is unzipped so that the "recipe" for the protein can be removed from the DNA. Yet the information cannot be removed from the DNA until a specific protein needed to unzip the DNA already exists. So which came first – the protein needed to unzip the DNA or the DNA information needed to make the unzipping protein? Both had to be present simultaneously. Could the existence of a Creator be made any more apparent at a molecular level?

God had to have created a pair of chickens first. Fertile eggs could then be laid and incubated. An egg can't hatch itself.

1. *Biological Information: New Perspectives,* edited by Robert Marks, et.al., World Scientific Publishing, 2013.

CENSORED GEOLOGY

During Charles Darwin's five-year stint as naturalist aboard the HMS Beagle (1831-1836), he had lots of time to ponder a copy of ***Principles of Geology*** by Charles Lyell. Lyell was a lawyer-turned-geologist who masterfully argued that the Bible could not be trusted as a source of truth concerning the history of our planet because huge periods of time and slow gradual processes had formed its geological features. This idea, still taught as a foundational principle in geology classes today, is known as uniformitarianism. It is the idea that small changes, over huge periods of time, account for the huge geologic features of our planet (such as the Grand Canyon).

The influence of this principle, and the belief in the reality of these huge time periods, laid the foundation for Darwin's belief that small biological changes, filtered by natural selection over huge periods of time, could account for the vast variety of life on our planet today.

This principle of slow gradual change over long periods of time has become so ingrained as a basis of geological interpretation that the evidence supporting its acceptance has long been forgotten, and the majority in geological sciences are totally unaware of evidence supporting any other viewpoint.

This section reveals some of the strongest geological evidence indicating that a global flood (commonly known as Noah's flood) did, indeed, occur upon the entire earth approximately 4,500 years ago. The reality of "Noah's Flood" has profound implications on the correct understanding of the vast majority of geological formations and sedimentary rock layers of our planet. This flood compresses the entire time frame of earth history and confirms straightforward statements from the Bible. The complexity of biological life leaves no other logical conclusion than "DESIGNER", but it is the evidence from geology (fossils, coal seams, and geological features) which accurately reveals the true age of these different biological creatures.

Buried Alive!

Evolution supposedly happened as mutations changed one creature into a completely different type over unfathomable eons of time. Each generation of dead carcasses was supposedly left to decay as sediment took enormous amounts of time to settle around any remains which did not get picked apart by scavengers and the forces of nature. The fossil record supposedly shows this slow modification of one creature into a different kind, and the depth of sediment surrounding these dead creatures supposedly represents enormous amounts of time … time … and more time. The core of evolution is the belief in enormous periods of time to explain everything from rock formations to life's development. Does the fossil record really reveal these huge periods of time and slow gradual burial, or is there a better explanation?

An estimated 100 million buffalo were slaughtered and their carcasses left to rot and decay upon the Great Plains from 1820 and 1880; yet there are no undisputed examples of fossilized Great Plains buffalo bones from this mass carnage because the remains were not rapidly buried by flood waters and sediment. Fish die by the millions during red tide events; yet every cell of these fish end up as food for other sea creatures - no new fossils form. When clams die, their muscles relax and the two half shells always open up, often to be ground into sand by the actions of wave and surf; yet many fossilized bivalves (clams) are found around the world buried so rapidly and deeply that they had no time either to burrow out or to open up. The fossil record is replete with organisms displaying evidence of rapid water burial:

- The vast Green River fine limestone formation in Wyoming contains swamp creatures such as turtles and alligators; fresh water fish such as sunfish and pickerel; salt water creatures such as deep sea bass, mollusks, and crustaceans; and land animals such as mammals and birds. How did animals from such a wide variety of habitats come to be buried together?

- Fossil Bluff in Tasmania contains over a thousand different types of sea creatures (such as whales) but also contains creatures as far removed from ocean life as possums. How did a whale come to be buried with a possum?

- One hundred thousand individual fossil specimens representing 400 different species, including ferns, scorpions, marine creatures, insects, reptiles, and amphibians have been identified within the shale beds of Mazon Creek near Chicago. What kept these vast numbers and types of creatures from being consumed before burial? Why are their remains so clearly identifiable?

- Millions of soft body jellyfish fossils have been found within a 400-square-mile sandstone bed in South Australia. Dead jellyfish melt in the sun and are rapidly destroyed by crashing waves. How did these creatures become so exquisitely preserved?

- Examples of fossils in the very act of giving birth or eating other fish have been found within fossil beds. How can this be explained by evolution's slow, gradual formation of fossil beds?

These are just a few examples indicating that the entire fossil record is a result of rapid burial processes.[1] These characteristics of the fossils - there for anyone to observe from locations around the world - scream out "rapid burial" of the enormous quantities of plants and animals preserved in the rocks. This is exactly the evidence we would expect to find through the action of a world-covering flood catastrophe and its aftermath.

1. *The World's a Graveyard*, Andrew Snelling, *Answers Magazine*, Vol. 3 No. 2, June 2008.

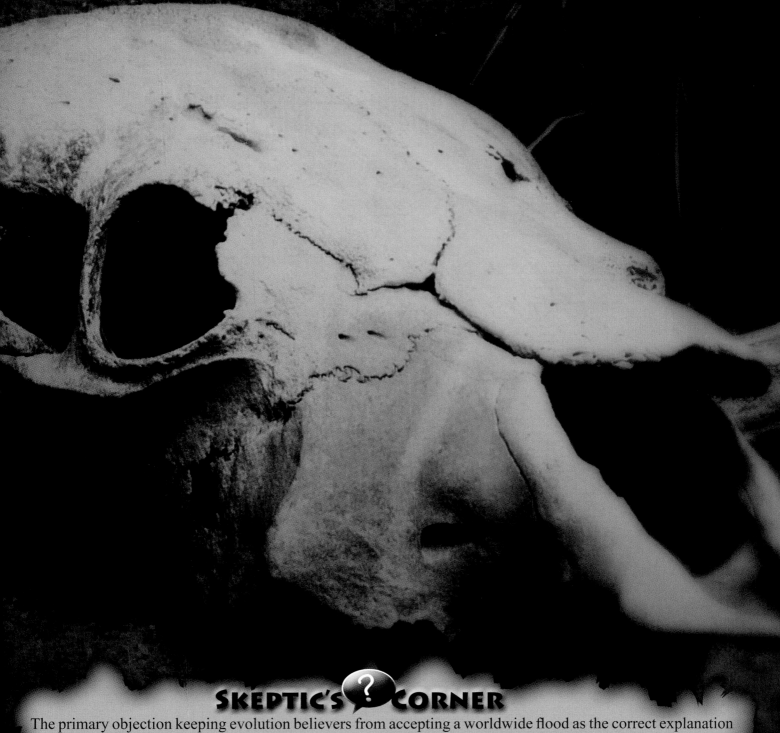

SKEPTIC'S ❓ CORNER

The primary objection keeping evolution believers from accepting a worldwide flood as the correct explanation for the fossil record is not that the evidence from sedimentary rocks does not match the characteristics which would be expected from such an event. Rather, the biggest problem for evolution believers is that such a flood explains the fossil record within too brief a span of time - an interval of a single year only a few thousand years ago. [Note: A small portion of the fossil record may be a consequence of post-flood catastrophism, but the vast majority must have been formed during the year-long flood of Noah.] The central article of faith for evolution believers is neither mutations nor natural selection because both have enormous difficulties in explaining the upward advancement in life's complexity. The non-negotiable core of evolution is the belief in an immense age for the earth. Without this foundation, all excuses for rejecting the reality of a personal Creator God evaporate. The rapid burial of enormous numbers of creatures during the worldwide flood eliminate entirely the need for huge periods of time in explaining the rock and fossil record. Consideration of a worldwide flood, even though it provides great explanatory power for understanding sedimentary rock layers, is therefore vigorously suppressed. Evolutionary geologists accept many "local flood" events, but they insert enormous periods of time between these obviously flood-produced layers.

God of the Gaps

My children's favorite read-aloud books were a two-volume set of stories by Robert McCloskey called **Homer Price** and **Centerburg Tales**. Several of these stories involved the tall tales told by Homer's Grandpa Hercules. In one of these stories Grandpa Herc was panning for gold in "ol' Californy," and his partner Hopper routinely put the gold nuggets in his pockets while hopping back and forth across the stream. Gold, "being powerful heavy," weighted Hopper down as he hopped back and forth over the stream, carrying his tremendously increasing weight. One day Hopper decided to take a bath in the stream and took off all his clothes (containing the heavy load of gold nuggets). He shed so much weight so suddenly that when he hopped over the stream he sailed several hundred feet into the air and became stranded at the top of the cliff overlooking the valley.[1]

The basic concept driving this tall tale is that small changes over time can make an enormous difference in a person's ability to perform athletic feats. The basic concept of evolution is that small changes over time can eventually change one type of creature into a completely different type of creature. Creation-believing Christians often find themselves arguing over the effect of small changes, rather than pointing out the enormity of the "hundred-foot-leap-onto-a-cliff"-type gaps which exist between very different types of creatures.

The simplest creature is the bacterium. There is such an enormous leap between the chemicals which make up a bacterium and any living bacterium that no experiment has ever shown how chemicals could "become" a bacterium. This is the first hundred-foot gulf which no amount of small one-change-at-a-time additions of chemicals can bridge.

Life itself is divided into three enormous groupings - Bacteria, Archaea (simliar to bacteria having no cell nucleus but different enough to be put in a new classification), and Eukarya (all forms of life having a cell nucleus). Saying something from one of these broad groups turned into something in the other group is akin to believing that an athlete training with ankle weights could run a two minute mile upon shedding the weights.

There are also enormous leaps between the energy conversion mechanisms used by different classes of creatures. Animals eat (ingest), fungi absorb, and plants convert sunlight (photosynthesis). Some creatures love extreme pressure which would kill all other creatures (barophiles), some thrive in temperatures near boiling which would fry all other creatures (thermophiles) and some love the acidity of fuming sulfuric acid (acidophiles). Each of these creatures is so different that the transition from one to the other is less feasible than a baseball player, training with weighted bats, becoming capable of hitting a ball out of New York's Yankee Stadium all the way into the Chicago Cub's Stadium.

Even animals within the same phyla (very broad basic body types) exhibit enormous gaps between very different types. For instance, all creatures with a backbone are grouped into one phylum; yet turtles have shoulder blades positioned completely different from all other reptiles - with no known transition. Bats are completely different in body structure from any other mammal, to the point that a working transition is difficult even to imagine, and nothing has ever been found in the fossil record linking these very different groups.[2] For some reptile to have turned into a turtle or some small rodent to have turned into a bat would be akin to a weightlifter training with five-hundred-pound weights in order to lift the Empire State Building.

Evolution promotes many more "hundred-foot-leap-onto-a-cliff" transitions between animals, yet all are as fanciful as Robert McCloskey's stories. Still they are presented within our schools and museums as reality and science. There is enormous variety and continuity of life on earth; there are also thousands of enormous gaps. It is those enormous gaps between very different kinds of creatures which most strongly testify to the reality that it was a Creator (in essence the God of the Gaps) who placed all life upon this planet.

1. *Centerburg Tales*, Robert McCloskey, Penguin Books, 1979.
2. *The Discontinuity of Life*, Kurt Wise, **Answers Magazine**, Vol. 4 No. 1, Mar. 2009.

SKEPTIC'S ? CORNER

It is possible to find creatures with characteristics which seem to be "in-between" other creatures. A highly publicized example is a "transitional" creature called Tiktaalik, which has bones in its front fins, gills like a fish, and a head similar to a crocodile. As usual, the media went ballistic over this find with claims that a missing link bewteen fish and reptiles had been found; yet there are fish today which breathe air and drown if held below water, fish which have bones in their front fins, and fish which pull themselves over mud, using their fins. Claiming that any of these fish are transitional between fish and land animals is like claiming a platypus is transitional between a duck and a beaver because it has a bill like a duck and a tail like a beaver. Furthermore, subsequent to the find of Tiktaalik, fully formed reptiles found in lower rock layers proved that this creature could not have been the link between the two very different classifications of creatures.

There has been an enormous variety of fish in earth history (almost all of which are now extinct), so it should be no surprise that amongst this wide variety some creatures would surface with "in-between features." Using creatures such as Tiktaalik to explain the enormous gaps between different classes of creatures is as illogical as Grandpa Herc's story of his friend Hopper jumping hundreds of feet onto a cliff because he unloaded gold from his pockets.

Let's Fold A Mountain

Try any variation of the following experiment: Take your best china platter and bend it into a "U" shape. Whether the china plate is surrounded by pillows or boards, protected by steel plates, or encapsulated in plastic; whether the bending force is exerted excruciatingly slowly or rapidly; whether the plate had been soaked in water for a hundred years or recently dried – the plate will break, shatter, and fragment upon being forced out of shape. Rock behaves exactly like this fine china. When bent, it breaks.

Throughout the mountain ranges of the world there are enormous layers of sediment which have been bent and folded without breaking. This could only happen if these mountains were uplifted while the sediment were still of a soft, pliable, mud-like consistency. Yet we are told that the sediment making up these mountains hardened into rock hundreds of millions of years BEFORE the mountains were uplifted. This folded sediment is an enormous mystery for the evolutionary viewpoint but no problem for the Biblical creation model. So how do believers in evolution account for these unbroken seams of sediment?

When unbroken, bent sediment layers are found, evolutionary geologists assume these layers were bent deep with the earth as the layers were thrust upward by tremendous forces. They theorize that because the layers were restrained during this deformation process the inside bend of a curved sediment layer was compressed while the outside of a bend was left uncompressed. Evolutionary geologists assume that this allowed the hardened rock layer to bend without fracturing.

In the biblical model, huge regional layers of sediment were laid down horizontally under water, as one type of sediment sorted and rapidly accumulated on top of another during the geological event commonly known as Noah's Flood. This flood of 4500 years ago lasted for over a year with reverberations lasting for decades, if not centuries. The global catastrophe was accompanied by massive and rapid movement of the continental plates which pushed up the mountains both during and subsequent to the flood. Thus, it is not at all surprising that there would be soft, folded sediment layers visible within these uplifted mountain chains because the mountains were rising while the sediment was still soft. If this biblical model is correct, the Earth's sedimentary rock layers formed rapidly and recently.

CALICO, NEVADA MOUNTAINS

FEGGEKLIT, DENMARK - FUR FORMATION, ICE AGE DEFORMATION

A simple test can be used to determine which of these explanations is the truth: measuring the structure and density of the rock layers. If these bent sediment layers are the result of enormous pressures deep within the earth, then there would be a compression of the lower edge of a curved layer as it was bent. Both the structure and the density of such a bent rock layer would differ significantly from top to bottom. However, this is not the case. Such layers are relatively uniform regardless of where the samples are taken – indicating the material was bent while still soft. This bending of soft material means compression of the bottom surface would be accompanied by material redistribution within the layer. A good analogy would be the bending of wet clay verse bending of a china plate. Since no structural or density variations are found in these rock layers, millions of years could not possibly be involved in their formation because they must have been soft when deformed.

Evolution needs millions of years of earth history to seem believable. The biblical model explains the rock layers without resorting to long time periods. Were it not for the need to explain our existence without God's intervention (i.e. without an acknowledgement of Noah's flood as a real event of history), these folded rock layers would immediately be acknowledged as having been bent while still soft and pliable. Evolutionary presuppositions are actually a detriment to truth. It is the Biblical creation model which acknowledges actual scientific observations and provides the best explanation for the geological features of our planet.

ENGLAND – SEDIMENT LAYERS FOLDED BY COLLISION OF THE AFRICAN AND EUROPEAN PLATES

CANADIAN ROCKIES – FOLDED SEDIMENTARY ROCK LAYERS

HIMALAYA MOUNTAINS

WESTERN CAPE PROVINCE, SOUTH AFRICA – FOLDED SANDSTONE

Seashells and Seesaws

How did seashells get trapped into rock layers thousands of feet above sea level? Rocks at the top of the world's highest mountains contain billions of fossilized sea creatures. Obviously, even the sediments on mountain peaks were once deposited by water. The biblical creation model explains this as a result of the year-long flood of Noah. This flood wiped out vast numbers of sea creatures which became buried in rock layers (sometimes miles deep), and the sediments containing these sea creatures were uplifted into the earth's mountain chains at the end of this worldwide flood. The evolution model also acknowledges the uplifting of mountains but requires enormous amounts of time between the deposition of the various layers. This evolution story adds billions of years of slow deposition and requires over a dozen up-and-down movements of enormous continent-sized land surfaces.

Which story is true?

The most revealing evidence comes from the way each model explains the many sedimentary (water-deposited) layers of rock which form the mountains. Evolution assumes that continent-size rock layers formed as "sediments were deposited during successive transgressions and regressions of the sea." Yet some rock layers can be traced as a continuous layer extending all the way from Ireland to Australia - indicating that land areas half the diameter of the entire globe had to drop uniformly below the sea only to be raised up uniformly again millions of years later. Incredibly, if this evolutionary time-scale is to be believed, this seesaw action happened not once, but many times throughout Earth history.

Support for this repeated up-and-down, continent-sized land movement comes from two primary observations. The father of modern geology, Charles Lyell, was looking for a way to explain sea creatures high upon the land surface without acknowledging the reality of a worldwide flood. In 1830 he discovered that the columns of the Roman Temple of Serapis at Pozzuoli, Italy had evidence of sea-dwelling crustaceans twenty feet above sea level. Historical records indicated that the temple had sunk below the sea in the third century and had rapidly risen again in 1538 following a local volcanic event. This evidence was considered so significant that it was prominently featured in all twelve editions of *Principles of Geology*. The second evidence was an observation by Charles Darwin that an area "twice the size of the Black Sea" had risen up to fifteen feet during an earthquake in Concepcion, Chile. These two observations were promoted as proof that Noah's flood never happened and that entire continents have repeatedly sunk and risen below sea level, thereby explaining enormous regionally deposited layers of fossil within twenty-one strata layers around the globe.[1]

SKEPTIC'S CORNER

Uniformitarianism is the belief that current slow and gradual processes explain the geological features of our planet. Almost every geology or earth science book makes some sort of claim that sea fossils high above sea level are due to "sediments deposited during successive transgressions and regressions of the sea." Yet any mechanism explaining how this could have happened is vague, at best.

The enormous extent of regional sediment layers would require that entire continents remain as flat as billiard tables throughout the submersion and for millions of subsequent years. There is nothing similar anywhere on the planet today. To believe the same thing happened over a dozen times stretches belief beyond the breaking point. Minuscule changes in land level in localized geologically active areas simply do not explain how almost identical sediment layers came to extend across multiple continents.

The primary evolutionary explanation for the supposedly repeated rise and fall of sea level throughout history is a "fluctuation in sea floor spread rate". As this theory goes, when a new sea floor is rapidly spreading the average temperature of the sea floor rock is higher; which means the rock layers are less dense; which means they displace more water onto land surfaces; which would cause the seas to rise over the continents. This complex scenario of massive sea floor volume fluctuation is believed to have happened approximately twenty-one times through different epochs of earth history.

Alternatively, there is a much more straightforward and simple explanation for the flooding of the continents. During the year-long flood of Noah, there would have been rapid movement of tectonic plates with the pre-flood sea floor rapidly sliding into the earth's interior like a conveyor belt. This tumultuous process temporarily caused the ocean basins to shallow, the sea level to rise, and the continent surface to be deformed in a dramatic fashion. This resulted in layer after layer of new sediments depositing rapidly and sequentially on the submerged land surface. At the end of the flood, zones where the buoyant continental crust had been significantly thickened (mostly near the edges of the continents) bobbed up like a cork to form the spectacular mountain chains we see today.

The flood of Noah's time was a "once-in-history-event" which explains the fossil and sedimentary rock layers of the planet very well. It also explains the current characteristics of the ocean floor and the appearance of the earth's mountain chains.

The evolutionary belief in "see-saw-like" up-again, down-again submersions of entire continent-sized areas, twenty-one different times, seems to be quite a credibility stretch. This belief is based on very tenuous observational evidence in extremely small localized areas. There has never been any observation of the required continent-size movement of uniform sheets of sediment. Thus old-age geology is based on belief in evolution and its accompanying requirement of an enormous time frame - not scientific observation.

1. In the Minds of Men, Ian Taylor, TFE Publications, 2008.

INSTANT GEOLOGY

Could a single landslide rewrite two centuries of misconception? Modern geological thought is ruled by the axiom that "the present is the key to the past." In other words, the slow gradual processes of today indicate that huge periods of time have been required to produce the grandiose canyons, extensive coal seams, massive

SKEPTIC'S CORNER

What is the skeptic's response to this physical model of rapid coal formation, layered sedimentation, and river valley formation? They say the model is too localized to explain the huge sedimentary rock layers of the planet. Yet all models are small-scale, and the events at Mt. St. Helens reflect the type of events which occurred on a global scale during the worldwide flood. Skeptics also claim the river valley erosion happened while the sediment was still soft, so it does not explain the formation of larger formations such as the Grand Canyon. Yet the sediment formed at Mt. St. Helens had hardened into many distinct layers of rock long before the water carved out the 600-foot-deep canyon in the North Fork of the Toutle River. Hard rock erosion also took place in Step Canyon and Lookout Canyon during this flood flow event. Mt. St. Helens clearly shows how the processes operating during the worldwide flood could explain the geology of our planet.

RAPID FORMATION OF COAL BEDS

The standard explanation for the worldwide distribution of coal seams is that millions of years ago there were swamps covering much of the earth. However, coal seams are layered in nature and this appearance does not match the character of typical swamp sediments. After the eruption at Mt. St. Helens, a million uprooted trees were left floating on Spirit Lake. Over the next several years much of this vegetation mat sunk, resulting in layered organic-rich sediment on the bottom of Spirit Lake. All that would be required to turn this sediment into a layered coal seam would be rapid burial under high pressures and temperature, i.e., another volcanic event. This small scale model shows how a worldwide flood would have uprooted vegetation across the entire planet to produce layered coal seams over widespread areas.

WORLD WIDE DEVASTATION

Look at the devastation from this single eruption, still apparent decades after the top of Mt. St. Helens slid into the adjacent valley. During the worldwide flood the Bible states that "all the fountains of the great deep were broken…." (Genesis 7:11) This likely involved thousands of massive volcanic events. The entire earth would have been left looking like this scene in the aftermath of the earth-reshaping catastrophe of approximately 4,500 years ago. No wonder Noah remained on the ark for more than seven months after it landed on the mountains of Ararat. Yet in geologic significance, what happened at Mt. St. Helens was a minuscule event. Although the force of the eruption was greater than that of dropping an atomic bomb on Hiroshima every second for over

sedimentary rock formations, and enormous fossil beds of our planet. The explosion and accompanying flood flow at Mt. St. Helens, shows how "slow and gradual" is not necessarily the correct interpretation of the evidence.

SORTED HORIZONTAL SEDIMENT AND RAPID FORMATION OF NEW RIVER VALLEYS

four hours, the Mt. St. Helens eruption was 20 times smaller than the 1883 volcanic eruption on the island of Krakatoa in the South Pacific. The Krakatoa eruption caused the summer temperatures in Europe to be lower than the normal winter temperatures and lowered the average temperature on our entire planet for the next four years!

Just as God provided a path of escape from the judgement of the flood for Noah and his family, God has provided a way for us to return to fellowship with Him - through the sacrifice of Jesus Christ as payment for our rebellion.

When Mt. St. Helens erupted in May of 1980, the top third of the mountain was instantly fluidized by the tremendous force and heat of the trapped gases. Four billion cubic yards of material flowed at speeds estimated at over 150 miles per hour into the valley, laying down sediment up to 600 feet deep. Over the next several months, rain water backed up until it broke through the recently consolidated rock layers to create completely new river valleys, transforming the landscape within hours. These new river valleys did not form over millions of years by slow erosion processes. To the amazement of scientists, these catastrophically formed strata (especially in

the newly formed North Fork Toutle River canyon), exhibited finely sorted horizontal layers of materials. These horizontal rock layers did not develop over long time periods but formed from sediments which rapidly flowed into place. The same sort of regional horizontal layers of sedimentary rock, which can be seen around the world, is simply the result of a much larger flood on a worldwide scale.

DINOSAURS AND BIBLICAL HISTORY

One of the most frequently asked questions when talking about biblical creation has to do with dinosaurs. Our culture has been repeatedly indoctrinated with the idea that dinosaurs roamed the earth for 160 million years - only to go extinct about 65 million years ago. This story is so ingrained that even preschool children can parrot it as a fact. So where do we put this "fact" into biblical history?

There is a growing body of intriguing evidence demonstrating that dinosaurs did not die out millions of years before man existed but that ancient cultures were keenly aware of these majestic beasts. Here are just a few observations:

- The word *dinosaur* was not invented until 1841, following the discovery of several extinct reptiles in England that appeared to walk erect, including *Iguanodon* and *Megalosaurus*. Predating these finds, cultures all over the world, from Egypt to England, from Greece to China, have a rich heritage of accounts describing dinosaur-like creatures commonly referred to as "dragons." Why is this knowledge so widespread if dinosaurs have, in fact, been extinct for millions of years?

- The Bible has more details in Genesis (the first book) about a world-covering, global restructuring flood than about creation itself. This event buried plants and animals by the trillions, resulting in most of the sedimentary rock layers and coal seams containing fossils. Almost every dinosaur fossil is found in "sedimentary rock" (laid down rapidly - under water).

- The account of an individual family (Noah) and a floating vessel as a method of preserving life during this flood can be found in the recorded and verbal history of over one hundred different cultures around the world. Because many of the cultural accounts and artifacts revealing dinosaur activity date from after this worldwide flood, it seems evident that young representative dinosaurs must also have been taken aboard this vessel. Thus knowledge of them would go with the different human cultures which spread out over the world after the flood. This is what we find.

Peruvian Ica Stone depicting dinosaur and man
To the right is a picture of an actual, less than 2,000-year-old, Ica burial stone found in Peru. Because a small percentage of these stones depict man with dinosaurs, and because some modern counterfeits have been produced, skeptics reject all of the dinosaur-picturing stones as fakes. Yet modern fakes are easily recognized by the lack of patina (an oxidation which takes time to develop upon the surface) in the cut grooves. A missionary mentions the stones in 1535 and some were sent to Spain in 1563 – all prior to the "discovery of dinosaurs" in the 1800's. Stones have also been documented to have been removed directly from tombs and to have passed many tests of authenticity.

Petroglyph in Natural Bridges National Monument, Utah
This rock drawing by Native Americans indicates a knowledge of dinosaurs long before Western explorers "discovered" America.

• There are hundreds of cave drawings, literature descriptions, burial stones, pottery, ancient temple depictions, and even passages in the Bible (Job 40:15-24, 41:1-34) which describe details that clearly fit what we know about the appearance, habitat, and behavior of dinosaurs. These all date from after Noah's flood.

It is not any single example of ancient mankind's knowledge of dinosaurs, but the breadth and variety of examples, which imply that man has, indeed, interacted with these creatures. It is only the denial of a worldwide flood which prevents modern science from accepting the reality of the co-existence of man and dinosaurs.

SKEPTIC'S ? CORNER

When presented with the type of evidence shown on this page, skeptics will always reject it as fake or misinterpreted. To do otherwise would cause the collapse of the belief in millions of years of earth history, and with this collapse goes the belief in evolution as the correct explanation for the existence of life. Skeptics must maintain a gap separating dinosaurs and man in order to maintain the belief in an ancient age of the rock layers. This provides naturalists with the long time periods needed for evolution. Therefore, in spite of clear evidence that people have seen dinosaurs, skeptics will simply choose to believe that these types of artifacts do not represent real dinosaurs or were not produced by ancient people. Microbe-to-man evolution is dogma rather than science, so no amount of evidence indicating that man and dinosaurs co-existed will convince evolution believers of this fact.

Bas-relief dinosaur in the ruins of Angkor outside of Siem Reap, Cambodia
This depiction of a dinosaur was found on an eleventh-century temple in Cambodia accurately drawn, yet it was only in the past 50 years that scientists figured out how this dinosaur looked. Above and below this carving are depictions of monkeys, birds, reptiles and other real creatures.

Carlisle Cathedral in Northern England
This 1496 brass relief of a dinosaur-type creature in an English cathedral is covered with a rug to prevent viewing. The declining church in England is so enamored with combining biblical history with Darwinism that they do not wish to display anything which would undermine the belief in evolution (with its required millions of years of earth history).

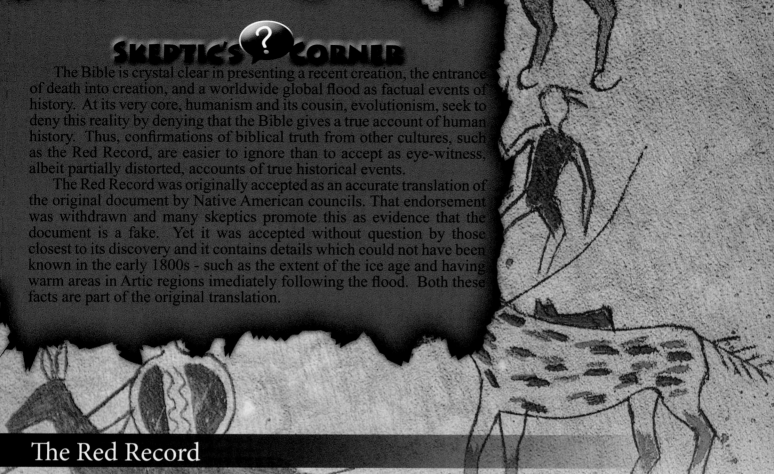

The Bible is crystal clear in presenting a recent creation, the entrance of death into creation, and a worldwide global flood as factual events of history. At its very core, humanism and its cousin, evolutionism, seek to deny this reality by denying that the Bible gives a true account of human history. Thus, confirmations of biblical truth from other cultures, such as the Red Record, are easier to ignore than to accept as eye-witness, albeit partially distorted, accounts of true historical events.

The Red Record was originally accepted as an accurate translation of the original document by Native American councils. That endorsement was withdrawn and many skeptics promote this as evidence that the document is a fake. Yet it was accepted without question by those closest to its discovery and it contains details which could not have been known in the early 1800s - such as the extent of the ice age and having warm areas in Artic regions imediately following the flood. Both these facts are part of the original translation.

The Red Record

The first question asked by someone upon awakening from a coma is, "How long have I been asleep?" When told they have been sleeping for weeks, or even years, the response is disbelief and skepticism; however, when a second source (such as a newspaper) reveals the same information, it is much more likely to be accepted as the truth. Having two independent sources confirming the same information more than doubles your confidence that you have, indeed, been given the truth. In a straightforward, factual way the Bible lays out key concepts of history:

- *The Bible is not a biology textbook* but it states ten times in the first chapter that diverse types of creatures have been created to reproduce "after their own kind."

- *The Bible is not a psychology textbook* but it describes human beings as universally guilty, bringing death upon themselves by choosing disobedience to their Maker. God cursed all of creation with death so that we would not live for eternity separated from Him. On the other hand, the Bible describes Adam and Eve as originally created in the image of God and designed to live forever in fellowship with God.

- *The Bible is not a geology textbook* but describes a world-covering flood taking place several thousands of years ago which would have been directly responsible for most of earth's fossils, sedimentary rock layers, coal seams, river valleys, mountain ranges, and the one great ice age. Moreover, the Bible indicates the earth was originally formed "out of water" (2 Peter 3:5).

- *The Bible is not a world history textbook* but describes the dispersion of different people groups, some of which would have crossed over the Bering land bridge into Alaska and North America during the ice age after leaving the Tower of Babel. It seems logical that people would have taken with them an oral and written tradition describing all of these great events of human history. This is exactly what was preserved in the "Wallam Olum" (The Red Record) of the "Lenni Lenape" (original people), commonly known as the Delaware Indian Tribe.

The Delaware Indians are widely regarded as having the oldest and most accurate account of all North American ancestral records. A carved wooden copy of the Red Record (the most valuable possession of a Delaware record-keeper) was given to Dr. Ward as a thank-you for saving the remnants of their tribe from an epidemic in 1820. In 1822, Dr. Ward passed this written record on to Constantine Rafinesque, a college professor who spent the next fifteen

years meticulously translating the document. The parallels between this document and the Bible are astounding, but because it was first translated at a time in American history when Native Americans were considered savages, a document describing their knowledge of history which predates biblical revelation was not necessarily welcomed with open arms. A century and a half passed before the document resurfaced.

So what does this written record of history describe? Later sections provide a detailed description of the ancient Delaware ancestral journey through Siberia, across the Bering Land Strait, through Alaska and the Pacific Northwest, and spreading eastward throughout North America. Such details place the origins of the document at greater than four thousand years ago, making the Red Record concurrent with the oldest books in the Bible, such as Genesis and Job.[1]

The Red Record begins by describing the Great Spirit creating everything from a swirling chaos of water. Land was separated from the waters, and distinctly different types of creatures were formed next. Last to be created was a man … followed by a woman. People lived in harmony with each other and were created immortal, meant to live forever. Evil and turmoil entered this world only after a snake brought corruption into creation. Things deteriorated until a great flood came "flooding and flooding; filling and filling; smashing and smashing; drowning and drowning." The ancestor to all the Delaware people, named Nenabush, built a vessel to bring their people through the great flood. Subsequent to this unforgettable event, their people migrated through great fields of ice to North America.[2]

There are obvious discrepancies between this Native American account of creation/early earth history and that given by the Bible. But the agreement with key events is startlingly apparent. How could two completely different cultures - separated by more than a hundred generations, thousands of years, and over ten thousand miles - have such similarity unless the two people groups shared a common rememberance of their early history? The obvious answer is that the ancestors of the American Indians and the ancestors of Abraham both left from the Middle East after the Tower of Babel and migrated to their respective locations after the great flood. Noah and Nenabush are different names for the same common ancestor of all mankind. Both the Bible and the Red Record document the same key events of human history - creation, the fall of mankind, and a worldwide flood - because these events actually happened.

1. Note: Pictured above is an early buckskin drawing of Indians on horseback. Horses were introduced to America by the Spanish in the 1500's. The original Wallam Olum has been lost but goes on to describe the trek across the Pacific Northwest and American continent on foot.
2. *The Red Record (The Wallam Olum): The Oldest Native North American History*, Translated and Annotated by David McCutchen, Avery Publishing Group, 1993.

Towers of Missing Time

For almost 200 years, students of earth science have been taught to interpret the earth's rock layers guided by the assumption of uniformitarianism. This guiding belief of geology assumes that slow gradual processes can account for the earth's grandiose features and thick rock layers. In other words, small changes over huge periods of time, it is claimed, explain the large effects we see.

Although uniformitarianism is still taught as a foundational principle of geology, the last few decades have seen a swing toward the acknowledgement that massive regional catastrophes may well correctly explain many, if not most, of the earth's widespread layers of sedimentary rock. This change in thinking is in no small part due to the efforts of creation geologists, who have shown that catastrophes are a better explanation for sedimentary rock layers. However, evolutionary geologists still cling to the idea that millions (in some cases tens of millions) of years have passed **BETWEEN** the deposition of successive layers.

To acknowledge that many successive layers were formed rapidly, one immediately following another, with relatively little time passing between the deposits, would essentially destroy any possibility that enough time had passed on earth to allow for one form of life to evolve into another. Therefore, as more and more layers of rock are acknowledged to have been deposited catastrophically (rather than being the

result of the slow, gradual settling of sediments), geologists trained to accept an extremely old earth must, logically, place the missing time between the layers.

This makes geological features which indicate that there was little, if any, "missing time" between the layers of deposition of extreme significance. Sandstone intrusions are such features.

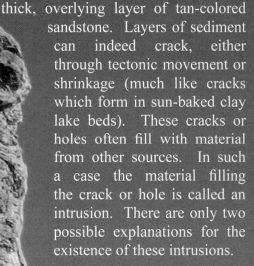

The picture on this page shows a column of white sandstone pushed up from below through a thick, overlying layer of tan-colored sandstone. Layers of sediment can indeed crack, either through tectonic movement or shrinkage (much like cracks which form in sun-baked clay lake beds). These cracks or holes often fill with material from other sources. In such a case the material filling the crack or hole is called an intrusion. There are only two possible explanations for the existence of these intrusions.

The first possibility is that the underlying sandstone was still fluid (filled with water) when the overlying rock layer settled on top of it. When the overlying layer was either depositied or moved into place, the excess weight caused the "still fluid layer" underneath to ooze up through the resulting holes and cracks, eventually hardening into the sandstone column. If the overlying layer was softer, it would eventually be eroded away, leaving the exposed white sandstone column shooting up into the air. If this is the correct explanation, then the particle size and distribution of the material in the column should be similar to the underlying sandstone layer. It also means the deposition of the upper, tan-colored sandstone had to have happened rapidly and before the underlying wet sandstone layer had time to harden into rock. Thus millions of years could not possibly have passed between the laying down of the two different rock layers.

The second possibility is that cracks developed in the tan-colored layer and that sand settled down into the cracks from above. In this case the cracks should be filled with sandstone with particle sizes and impurities different from those found in the layer below. Thus, the makeup of the sand within the sandstone intrusions reveal their origin and whether the subsequent sand layers were formed rapidly or whether great periods of time elapsed between.

In almost all cases where sandstone intrusions are present, the characteristics of the columns match the underlying sediment, showing that the column was produced from the underlying material while it was still soft and able to flow. This means that no great period of time passed before the lower layer was squeezed upward. It is difficult to imagine any condition which would maintain a layer of sand underneath trillions of pounds of overlying sediment for millions of years in a soft, uncemented state and able to flow. Sandstone intrusions are very strong evidence for the **rapid** accumulation of multiple layers of sediment. This straightforward observation indicates that millions of years simply did not elapse in-between the deposition of these thick layers of earth sediment. They were laid down rapidly, one after another, during the year-long flood of Noah.[1]

1. *The Young Earth: The Real History of the Earth – Past, Present, and Future*, Dr. John Morris, Master Books, November 2007.

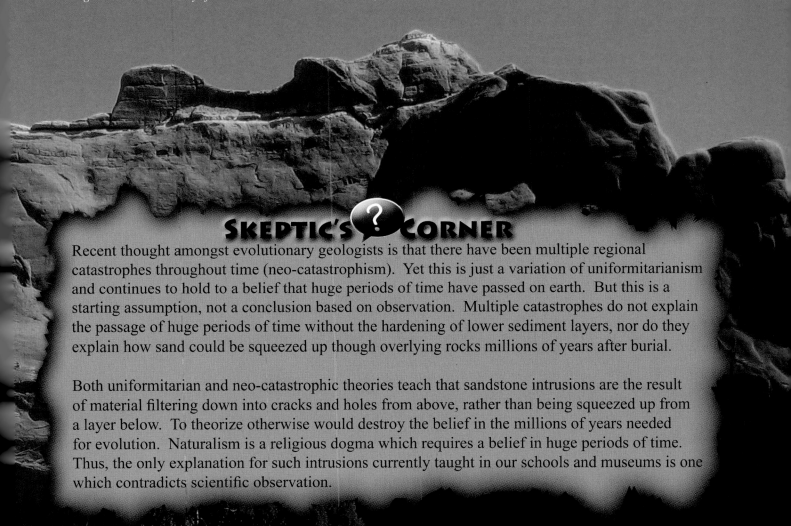

SKEPTIC'S CORNER

Recent thought amongst evolutionary geologists is that there have been multiple regional catastrophes throughout time (neo-catastrophism). Yet this is just a variation of uniformitarianism and continues to hold to a belief that huge periods of time have passed on earth. But this is a starting assumption, not a conclusion based on observation. Multiple catastrophes do not explain the passage of huge periods of time without the hardening of lower sediment layers, nor do they explain how sand could be squeezed up though overlying rocks millions of years after burial.

Both uniformitarian and neo-catastrophic theories teach that sandstone intrusions are the result of material filtering down into cracks and holes from above, rather than being squeezed up from a layer below. To theorize otherwise would destroy the belief in the millions of years needed for evolution. Naturalism is a religious dogma which requires a belief in huge periods of time. Thus, the only explanation for such intrusions currently taught in our schools and museums is one which contradicts scientific observation.

Flooded but not Forgotten

As explorers, traders, military conquerors, and missionaries have spread across the globe over the last two thousand years, they have encountered hundreds of unfamiliar cultures. Some of these cultures were highly advanced, while others were pitifully primitive. These outsiders documented the numerous cultural accounts of ancient events remembered by these many people groups. Amongst the most commonly recorded stories are those of humanity's origin. Now suppose that this compilation of historical records, received from widely diverse people groups from around the planet, revealed an account of humanity's origin via a strange traveler from the "sky, stars, or heavens" who had arrived on earth long ago in a vessel which flew through the air "like an eagle, falcon, snowflake, or falling star."

Trail sign on North Rim of Grand Canyon

The movies today are filled with science fiction concepts of aliens which have visited the earth from outer space. Should such a concept as past alien visitation show up in historical records from peoples across the globe, it would be widely promoted as proof that aliens really did exist. Suppose various forms of this same story had showed up in over two hundred different cultures from around the planet - originating long before any of these cultures had closely communicated. Would not such a thread of common remembrance receive mention and analysis in books of world history?

There is such a body of common remembrance - not concerning visitors from outer space - but for an event of such overwhelming geological significance that its implications are mind-boggling. Yet this collection of eye-witness testimonies is seldom mentioned in world history books. The traditions preserved in a vast number of cultures concerns the common knowledge of a past flood of worldwide proportion. For instance, one non-Christian web site[1] lists 258 different cultural stories of a flood. Over ninety percent of these stories indicate that the flood was worldwide in extent, killing all humanity except a select "hero figure." Over seventy percent of the accounts mention that the flood was sent by some "god-like figure." Approximately fifty percent of the accounts include details indicating that the flood was sent in response to man's sinfulness, that the hero was saved along with a select few (often from his family), and that he was saved on some sort of floating vessel.

Twenty-five percent of the accounts, from cultures spanning the globe, specifically mention that animals were taken on the floating vessel and also saved. A significant number of accounts even mention that a rainbow was sent after the flood as a sign of hope; or that birds were sent out to see if the flood was over; or that the flood lasted for many months or even years.

All of this makes perfect sense if the global flood of Noah was a reality which happened several thousands of years ago, just as it is clearly recorded as a factual event of history in the Bible. People groups would have moved out from the Middle East subsequent to this world re-shaping catastrophe, taking with them an increasingly incomplete account of this pivotal event of human history. With time, different cultures would have developed slightly different versions of the real event, but the remembrance would be genuine and persisting. This is exactly what we find. Although this is not scientific proof of the reality of the worldwide flood, it is strong logical evidence for the reality of this world-reshaping event. It is this flood which explains the sedimentary rocks and fossils found across our planet without the necessity of adding huge amounts of time to Earth history. The widespread nature of these flood stories, from over 250 different cultures spread across the globe, testify to this flood as a real event in human history. The Bible provides the most straightforward and logical eyewitness account of the flood and the Bible has never been proven wrong on any of its straightforward statements concerning the history of our planet.

1. *Flood Stories from Around the World*, Mark Isaak, www.home.earthlink.net/~misaak/floods.htm, updated June 21, 2006

SKEPTIC'S CORNER

Skeptics dismiss ancient flood stories as imaginative exaggerations of local events. Remember when evaluating this viewpoint that it comes from a mindset devoted to the principle of naturalism. Naturalism depends on the rejection of any supernatural intervention in human history. In order to explain all of life without God, vast periods of time are required. A worldwide flood eliminates the need for such huge periods of time because it explains the rock and fossil record in terms of a single, intense year-long catastrophe only 4500 years ago. Thus rejection of a global water catastrophe is critical to maintaining the naturalist worldview and has led to ridicule of the flood as a real event of history. Yet why are the stories so often tied to judgment of mankind by God? Why are they so widespread in nature? Why is there not judgment by ice for the Eskimos, drought for the Egyptians, or earthquake for the Armenians? Why is humanity always saved by a single man on a floating vessel? The common remembrance of a real event in earth history explains the widespread nature and common themes of these flood accounts.

The Mystery of the Woolly Mammoths

Since the late 1800's, an estimated 60,000 ivory tusks have been recovered from the frozen northern tundra of Alaska, Canada, and Siberia. Undecayed mammoths have been found frozen and well-preserved enough to feed sled dogs. Semi-tropical vegetation has been found undecayed within the mammoth stomachs. Other mammoths are documented to have been so "quick frozen" that they are found partially standing in an upright position, often in mounds of dust turned into frozen mud. It is conservatively estimated that in the relatively recent past several million mammoths roamed the plains of northern Siberia - yet not one is alive today. Where do these animals fit into biblical history? What happened to wipe out millions of these magnificent creatures in a very short time period? How did their frozen, undecayed carcasses come to be encapsulated within the permanently frozen north? Why is there semi-tropical vegetation in their stomachs which could not possibly grow in this frozen wasteland? Why are many of the dead animals still standing in an upright position? The answer to these questions provides an important distinction between the evolutionary view of our planet and the biblical account of history.

The Bible describes a world-covering flood that occurred several thousand years ago. This event happened over an entire year-long period and was accompanied by massive volcanism, rapid continental movement, and enormous erosion and sediment deposition processes which significantly warmed the oceans of the world, causing mass extinctions. Water is a marvelous heat absorption medium, and this higher average water temperature (possibly as much as 30°F) resulted in enormously greater evaporation rates. This, in turn, resulted in storms, floods, rain, and snow on a worldwide scale which dwarfs anything we see occurring today. So much heat was contained within the ocean water that it took centuries for evaporation to cool the oceans to today's equilibrium temperature.

SKEPTIC'S CORNER

Skeptics have not been able to come up with a model of earth history that adequately explains either the cause of the ice age or the demise of the mammoths. All current naturalistic models use unrealistic assumptions and do not explain how so much water could have evaporated from the oceans to produce the huge ice sheets which covered much of Europe and North America. These models generally assume a cooler global ice age temperature, which implies lower, not higher, evaporation rates compared to today. The superior biblical model, which does explain these things in a very straightforward way, continues to be suppressed.

Meanwhile, billions of gallons of water were locked up as snow in Canada, Europe, Greenland, & Antarctica. The compacting and spreading of these snow sheets caused the ice age and resulting geological features.

Now let's look at what was happening to people and animals during this period of earth history. Animals released from Noah's ark rapidly propagated and moved out across the earth, filling environmental niches they found. If we started with a single pair of mammoth-type creatures and assume that their population only doubled every five years, it would have taken less than two centuries for the mammoth population in a given region to grow to more than one million creatures. Animals were forced outward from the Middle East in search of additional food sources as their numbers multiplied. At the same time as these herds were growing, great ice sheets were spreading across northern latitudes - as the warm ocean water continued to evaporate and fall as snow. Before these sheets of ice had blocked their path, the mammoths apparently found a temperate region of the planet in the plains of upper Siberia and migrated across the Bering Land strait into the Canadian region adjacent to the Arctic Ocean and the Bering Sea. Because the oceans were still warm, these regions of the earth remained moderate in temperature even while huge sheets of ice were building up further to the south. This effectively isolated the mammoths to those areas relatively close to the ocean shore. Their population reached millions within this relatively temperate "climate bubble." Eventually the oceans cooled to the point that evaporation slowed, the Arctic Ocean and the Bering Sea completely froze over, and a dramatic and permanent climate change occurred upon our planet.

At this point, great regions of the planet which for centuries had experienced abundant rainfall became permanently drought-stricken and blanketed by airborne dust and volcanic ash. Meanwhile, the Arctic region (which had experienced summer-like weather year-round due to warming from temperate oceans) became a frozen tundra as ice permanently covered the adjacent ocean surface. Mammoths by the millions became trapped between the glaciers to the south and the frozen oceans to the north. At the same time, huge dust storms (possibly triggered by a huge volcanic event or large meteor strike) could have swept billions of pounds of volcanic ash and dust from dried lake beds into the air, and prevailing currents swept much of it into the north, burying mammoths as they suffocated in an upright standing position – then quickly freezing into a permanent standing position.[1]

This scenario explains all of the supposed mysteries of the frozen mammoths of the north. Sadly, this explanation is seldom presented to students because it depends upon a worldwide flood as the cause of the warmer oceans and recent ice age. Of course, this worldwide flood eliminates the need for huge time periods to explain both fossils and the development of life without God. Thus the explanation which best explains the mystery is simply ignored.

1. *Frozen in Time: The Woolly Mammoth, The Ice Age, and the Bible,* Michael Oard, Master Books, 2004.

The Sudden Appearance of Life

Over the last century science has been transformed from a study of how the world operates into a religion. This is a religion in which only natural causes are allowed to explain everything. Christianity offers an alternative worldview which acknowledges that the universe operates according to discoverable principles but also understands that God has interacted with His creation in the past. So which belief is correct, the narrower, naturalistic belief or the broader, Christian model? An examination of the first layer in the earth's rock record containing fossilized remains of multi-celled life provides an important clue.

In the naturalistic model, these rocks are a record of life's earliest development. Evolutionists teach that the Cambrian layer of rock is believed to have been laid down starting 540 million years ago. In the Biblical perspective these rocks represent the first sediment deposited during the worldwide flood at the time of Noah. In other words, the creatures trapped in this layer of rocks were simply organisms at the very earliest stages of this global catastrophe. These organisms are marine creatures from continental shelf environments, the very first organisms to be destroyed as tsunami-like waves progressively invaded the land surfaces.

If the biblical model is correct, you would not expect to find fossils of cattle or people buried with those of trilobites or coral because the vast diversity of creatures in the preflood world lived in highly diverse habitats at differing elevations above sea level and therefore would have been buried at different times and locations during the flood. In a given rock layer you would thus generally expect to find only the sorts of creatures from the habitat being destroyed at that moment during the flood and not a blurred continuum of life.

If naturalistic evolution is correct, then life must have started out as some form of single cell organism. Descendents from this organism must then have increased in their complexity to become a wide variety of multi-cellular organisms. Completely new functions and features somehow appeared. There must have been millions of unique intermediate forms as one type of creature gradually transformed into a distinct new type. Most mysterious and confounding of all, somehow sexual reproduction appeared as a single sex organism simultaneously turned into both a male and a female. What a magic trick!

So what does this lowest level of fossil-containing rock reveal? The Cambrian rock layer contains most of the major phyla (body types) of the world, including sponges, trilobites, brachiopods, jellyfish, crinoids, plankton, cephalopods, and a dizzying array of other creatures with an enormous variety of body structures, including fish with a backbone. This layer testifies to abrupt appearance, stasis (the same forms of life continuing into the present), and extreme complexity, even at the lowest strata levels. What better evidence for creation could there be?

If evolution is really true, how did a single-celled organism turn into a trilobite having extremely complex eyes and leave nothing in-between? No one knows. How did the hard shells of brachiopods form with nothing as an intermediate structure? No one knows. How did the enormously complex community of creatures known as coral form without any transitional structure? No one knows. So which model of reality fits this actual physical evidence: the sudden appearance of very diverse and complex forms of life (each without any in-between form linking the very different body structures), or the gradual modification of one body form into another?

Christianity is by its very nature dependent on the acknowledgement of God as an explanation of certain events in history. The creation of extremely wondrous and diverse forms of life is one of these events. Yet evolution is even more dependent on faith. There is no physical evidence for the slow development of the marvelous complex structures preserved in the Cambrian Period. To say that random mutations guided by natural selection produced them is little better than believing a magician pulled them out of a hat.

SKEPTIC'S CORNER

Skeptics attempt to deal with the damaging evidence to the theory of evolution from the Cambrian layer "explosion of life" by stretching the time frame during which these rocks supposedly were deposited. Yet this does not solve the problem of how a single-celled organism could possibly have turned into a wide variety of far more complex organisms without leaving any record of these multiple transformations within the rocks.

Another common response to the lack of fossil transitions is called "punctuated equilibrium." This supposedly explains the sudden change of one form of life into another (without any evidence in the fossil record) by stating that the change happened too rapidly or too localized to have left a record of the transition. This is claiming that the lack of evidence is actually evidence! The belief in single-cell-to-man evolution is faith, not science.

Mass Kill of Nautiloids in the Grand Canyon

The earth's crust can be likened to a huge wedding cake with different flavors of cake lying one atop another. The lower layers of rock are typically igneous rock (such as granite or basalt - a type of solidified lava) or metamorphic rock (such as gneiss or schist or marble), transformed from other kinds of rock by enormous heat and pressure. The upper layers are routinely sedimentary rock (such as limestone, sandstone, shale or coal), laid down underwater and later hardened into rock. It is the huge volume of these rock layers which has led to the belief that these rocks (whether igneous, metamorphic or sedimentary) took millions of years to form. Yet this is an assumption, not a fact. The rocks themselves do not talk, nor do they come with labels attached. They are simply interpreted in a manner consistent with the worldview of the interpreter.

One of the most striking rock layers in the Grand Canyon is the Redwall Limestone. This distinct layer of red rock ranges up to six hundred feet in thickness, covering over five thousand square miles of the western United States and extending into Utah, Colorado, Arizona, Nevada, and California. In actuality, the Redwall Limestone belongs to Mississippian groups which appear in many other places across North America as far as Tennessee and Pennsylvania. These limestones appear in exactly the same position in strata sequences with the same fossils and features. The widespread nature of such beds testify to the widespread nature of the flood which created them. The evolutionary worldview interprets this huge formation as having formed under a calm sea, 335 million years ago, as trillions of sea creatures died and settled excruciatingly slowly on the ocean floor as a limestone deposit. For hundreds of feet of compacted limestone to have formed in such a manner would require millions of years of earth history.

In 2002, Ph.D. geologist Steve Austin presented his case for a gigantic mass kill of ocean creatures called nautiloids entombed in a thin layer near the bottom of the Redwall Limestone. Nautiloids were similar to modern squid but lived inside of "sugar cone"-shaped shells up to four feet in length. There are several intriguing facts about these fossils. First, at the time Dr. Austin started studying these fossils, they were listed by the official Grand Canyon web site as extremely rare within the canyon - yet Austin had discovered hundreds of them over the years. Second, the creatures seemed to be concentrated only near the very center of a six-foot thick sub-layer within the Redwall Limestone. Third, once the location of the creatures within the rock layer was confirmed, it was discovered that they extended throughout that layer, across the full extent of the Grand Canyon and into Nevada to the west, with an estimated one billion creatures buried in all. Most significantly, Dr. Austin's measurements established that throughout the rock layer these cone-shaped shells were statistically aligned in one primary flow direction.

The significance of this find (which was reported at the 2002 Geological Society of America's annual conference[1]) is staggering. It can be shown that large cone-shaped objects suspended in sediment-laden fluid flowing in turbulent conditions would orient themselves roughly in a flow direction and essentially at the center of this turbulent layer. This is exactly the type of catastrophic flood flow deposition which would be expected in a world-wide flood of the type described in the Genesis account of the Bible. Thus, the discovery of a billion extinct squid-like creatures within this massive limestone layer, oriented in a single flow direction, is overwhelming evidence that one of the most distinct rock layers in the Grand Canyon was laid down rapidly and catastrophically, not slowly over millions of years.

If one of the most distinctive layers of limestone in the Grand Canyon was the result of rapid deposition by energetic flood waters, then there is little reason to cling to the idea that the other layers formed slowly and gradually - except that huge periods of time are needed to explain life's formation and development without God. It is the assumptions of evolution, not the facts of science, which cause people to believe that millions of years were required to form the sedimentary rock layers of our planet.

1. *Regionally Extensive Mass Kill of Large Orthocone Nautiloids, Redwall Limestone (Lower Mississippian), Grand Canyon National Park, Arizona*, Steve Austin, Presented at the GSA annual meeting, Denver, CO, Oct., 2002.

SKEPTIC'S CORNER

Uniformitarian assumptions simply do not explain the estimated one billion nautiloid fossils within the thin sub-layer of the Redwall Limestone layer which are statistically oriented throughout the entire deposit. It is obvious that a mass kill event occurred, but why the nautiloids should be oriented as if transported in a catastrophic underwater mudflow is not explained by the uniformitarian "tranquil sea" model for the limestone formation. The facts surrounding the nautiloid deposit both puzzle and amaze evolutionary geologists who missed this extensive layer because they were blinded by naturalistic assumptions of huge age and were not looking for so extraordinary a deposit.

A snowball in Hell

Growing up in Texas was hot. "Hotter than hell" was a common statement. One afternoon, a brother known for his pranks casually mentioned that he'd noticed a snowball lying outside on the previous day. He then strolled over to the door and bellowed in amazement, "It's still there!" His kid brother couldn't resist taking a look. Sure enough, sitting there as pretty as a glistening diamond on a green emerald carpet, was an unmelted snowball in the hot summer sun. He ran outside, touched its cold surface, looked for non-existent signs of melted ice, and pondered how a hunk of snow could remain for days in the blazing sun. That's when the prankster, who had just placed the snowball outside, clobbered his gullible brother with another snowball from the freezer.

Thousands of miles beneath the earth's crust, deep within the inferno of the earth, there exists a similar unmelted snowball in hell. To understand the implications of this find, you must first understand the biblical account of world history. The Bible unabashedly speaks of a worldwide flood as a real event of world history. This was not just a few days of hard rain but a geological catastrophe of global extent and staggering implications.

By comparing the sediments and types of fossils found on the ocean bottom today relative to those found on the continents, the evidence is overwhelming that the flood involved rapid movement of the earth's tectonic plates. In fact, the case is strong that none of the plates that underlay the ocean basins before the flood still exist at the earth's surface today, except for some tiny slivers that were thrust up onto the continents. The oceanic plates are huge slabs of cold, higher density rock which are resting upon hotter mantle rock beneath them. During this year-long flood event, the ocean plates apparently slid, like conveyor belts, into the hot mantle beneath. These preflood plates then plunged some 1800 miles from the earth's surface to the bottom of the mantle, where temperatures were at least 5,000°F (3,000°C) higher than at the surface.

Where the two plates pulled apart, new ocean floor was formed in the growing gap. This zone where two ocean plates have pulled apart is known as a mid-ocean ridge system. It runs like a baseball seam for some 40,000 miles around the earth and includes the Mid-Atlantic Ridge. It is within this zone where, during the flood, hot rock from the mantle melted and rose to fill the gap to form all of the ocean floor we have on the earth today.

During this tumultuous subduction process, the lighter continental plates bobbed up and down, submerging all land surfaces under water. Also, the molten rock filling the gaps along the mid-ocean ridge system vaporized enormous amounts of ocean water, forming spectacular jets of steam shooting into the upper atmosphere at supersonic speeds, carrying up massive volumes of water like huge fountains and producing rainfall around the globe which continued for "forty days and forty nights" - something on a scale never seen before or since.

If this were not enough, the cold plate material sliding into the earth's interior destabilized the earth's rotational behavior, causing the earth to temporarily flip over like a top. Enormous tsunami-like waves

SKEDTIC'S ? CORNER

This huge temperature difference simply could not be maintained over tens or hundreds of millions of years. Yet huge time periods are needed if evolution is to be believed. The main attempt to account for these observations has been to insist that the large differences in seismic wave speed must be primarily due to differences in chemical composition rather than temperature. In other words, instead of the lower mantle being well mixed chemically, there must be significant volumes of rock in the mantle that somehow have evaded the mixing process. But more than ten years of computer modeling attempts and hand-waving arguments have failed to produce any credible way to create and maintain the sort of chemical differences required.

swept over the continent surfaces, eroding and transporting huge amounts of sediment and depositing this sediment in layers thousands of miles across and in sequences thousands of feet thick. As the subduction ground to a halt, the natural buoyancy of the low density continents allowed them to rise above sea level, the flood water to drain into the deepening ocean basins, and enormous mountain chains to rise where the continental crust had been thickened by adjacent subduction - forming mountain chains such as the Andes, the Rockies, and the Himalayas.

The overall result of this earth-reshaping scenario would have been the destruction, rapid burial, and fossilization of the organisms which had been alive on the earth before the cataclysm; the formation of enormous beds of coal and oil deposits; the deposition of regional-scale sedimentary rock layers; a worldwide ice age driven by massive evaporation from warm oceans following the cataclysm; and an enormous mass of cold rock (from the pre-flood ocean floor) settling deep into the earth's super-hot mantle. All of these former characteristics are readily apparent as we observe the earth around us. But it is the last item (cold material deep within the mantle of the earth), which is especially revealing as to the accuracy of this interpretation of the earth's past.[1]

Such a region of cold material, nearly two thousand miles beneath the earth's surface, has been imaged for more than twenty years by seismic tomography.[2] This enormous mass of rock deep within the earth's mantle, located roughly beneath the perimeter of the Pacific Ocean where much of the subduction of the seafloor occurred, is estimated to be 3,000°C cooler than the surrounding mantle. If the subduction is as slow as evolutionists imagine, how could rock remain that cold during the roughly 100 million years it would take this material to reach the bottom of the mantle?

This observation of cold material deep within the earth's hot mantle makes sense only if the cold material plunged through the mantle recently – easily fitting into the biblical flood model. But any slow and gradual explanation, involving millions of years, makes as much sense as an unmelted snowball in hell.

1 *The Roles of Tectonics and Rotational Dynamics in the Genesis Flood*, John Baumgardner, Presentations of the Sixth International Conference on Creationism (Thursday evening lecture), Creation Science Fellowship, 2009.
2. *Mantle shear-wave tomography and the fate of subducted slabs*, Phil. Trans. R. Soc. London A, 360, 2475-2491, 2002.

A Real Jurassic Park?

On my way home from work one day, I drove past a plate of food placed alongside the road. I was surprised to observe how fresh and appetizing the rare, juicy filet seemed in the hot afternoon sun. On the second day, I slowed for a closer look, and the same plate of food looked just as appetizing as the previous afternoon. By the end of the week, the steak remained juicy and appetizing. Finally, after a month of passing the tantalizing meal, I stopped and helped myself to the succulent, undecaying, and wondrously delicious feast. A ridiculous story? Only because we all know that nothing can be left to the forces of time and nature without decaying.

In the Jurassic Park movies, scientists were able to bring dinosaurs back to life using DNA from amber-encased dinosaur blood. The problem not discussed in the movies is the rapid unzipping (deterioration) of biological molecules with time. It is only with the protection provided inside the cells of living organisms that the complex molecules of life can be maintained. DNA is so sensitive that it need only be placed in water to start degenerating.

All organic material, even when buried deep within bones, would be completely deteriorated within hundreds of thousands of years. Even if protected from environmental forces of water and erosion, natural radiation from radon gas and other sources would tear apart sensitive molecules over time. Thus, prior to 2005 no evolutionary scientist expected to find any intact organic tissue within dinosaur remains because they believed these bones to have been buried for at least sixty-five million years.

SKEPTIC'S CORNER

The response to this incredible find has been first to deny its authenticity, then, when careful observation made this impossible, to deny its significance by stating that the "model of how fossils form and organic tissues decay needs to be modified." In other words, evolutionists would rather rely on faith in future discoveries than accept the implications of a relatively recent burial. Once again, it becomes clear which model of reality is really resting on faith (evolution) and which rests on known observations (biblical creation).

Then, in 2005 Dr. Mary Schweitzer, assistant professor of paleontology at North Carolina State University, with a joint appointment at the NC Museum of Natural Sciences, dissolved some of the mineralized material away from a recently uncovered Tyrannosaurus rex bone. To her amazement, what appeared to be ligaments, blood vessels, and even undecayed blood cells were still present within the bone. This is not at all surprising if the dinosaur was buried as a result of a worldwide flood approximately 4,500 years ago. But if dinosaurs were buried sixty-five or more million years ago, this would be like finding a plate of undecayed food alongside the road after a month in the sun.

Naturalists claim that the rocks covering enormous areas of the western United States are thought to be hundreds of millions of years old, and that no dinosaur bones exist in sediment layers "dated" younger than 65 million years. So we are faced with a choice:

> a) The assumption that the rock layers are sixty-five million years old is wrong.
> b) Disregard what we know about the laws of physics and chemistry.

Evolutionists cannot discard their belief in enormous periods of time and remain evolutionists … so they will always choose "option b."

The discovery of the dinosaur tissue caused an enormous controversy within the scientific community because it simply shouldn't have been there. The initial response was to deny that the "still stretchy" tissue could actually be dinosaur remains. The fact that they show so little degradation "goes against everything we know about chemistry and physics."[1] Yet every test conducted since the initial find has confirmed that the tissue is genuine. Recently, Dr. Schweitzer's research team found a second dinosaur with "soft-tissue" structures like collagen and amino acids, confirming that the first discovery was not a fluke. This newest discovery of preserved "fossil proteins" was found in the femur of a duck-billed hadrosaur in Montana. There is still no good explanation for why it exists if these fossils are sixty-five million years old.[2,3]

If the biblical model of history is correct, the mystery is solved and no laws of science are violated - these bones were buried a mere few thousand years ago during Noah's flood and tissue inside the fossil bone had simply not yet totally fossilized. This is one of the many astounding evidences indicating that recent creation and the reality of a worldwide flood are the correct explanation of the rock and fossil record.

1. MSNBC interview with Dr. Schweitzer following the announcement of the find.
2. *Soft-Tissue Vessels and Cellular Preservation in Tyrannosaurus Rex*, Mary H. Schweitzer, March 25, 2005, *Science*, Vol. 307, no. 1952-1955, pp. 1852.
3. *Biomolecular Charactorization and Protein Sequences of the Campanian Hadrosaur B. Canadensis*, Mary H. Schweitzer, *Science*, May 1, 2009: Vol. 324, pp. 626-631.

Mr. Sandman

Criminals are often collared because they have left fingerprints or DNA fragments at the scene of the crime. A single fingerprint or fragment of DNA can pinpoint a particular person among billions of people on earth. In a similar way, minute trace chemicals form a fingerprint of a particular sandstone layer, differentiating its unique composition from any other rock. The chemical composition of a grain of sand can be unique enough to pinpoint its origin to a specific, sometimes distant, source region deposit formed at a particular time and place in history. But what does this have to do with the evidence for creation?

Foundational to the creation model is the reality of a worldwide flood. If this flood happened, it would have been energetic enough to have transported sediments, including enormous quantities of sand, across entire continents - resulting in local deposits of such sediments far removed from their original source. It turns out that this is exactly the case for many sandstone formations. For instance, the Navajo Sandstone deposit in southern Utah contains the same compositional fingerprint as sandstone layers from over 1,200 miles away in the Appalachian Mountains of Pennsylvania and New York. How could thousands of cubic miles of sand, deposited over hundreds of thousands of square miles, have been transported across the breadth of the country without leaving a trace of evidence in-between?

This mystery is analogous to finding the same DNA, from the same criminal, in apartments where people were murdered in New York and Los Angeles on the same day. How could the same person have committed the murder at such widely separated locations? If this story were placed in 1859, the mystery would be unsolvable, because there would be no method at that time for the murderer to have moved from New York to California in a single day. But if the crime had taken place in the twenty-first century, there would be no mystery because the villain could easily have traveled that far in one day. Thus it is the speed of transport which solves the mystery.

Similarly, if the sand were transported slowly from the Appalachian Mountains to the Rocky Mountains over huge periods of time, you would expect lots of changes in composition and size of the particles in the sand and evidence of sand deposition at many locations along the way. On the other hand, if the sand were moved rapidly by an enormously energetic flow of water, it could be held suspended and transported huge distances without mixing or dropping out of suspension at intermediate locations.[1]

This is exactly the type of energetic movement and sorting of massive amounts of sediment which would be expected during a worldwide flood. A global flood would result in the massive erosion and movement of sand from one area of the globe and subsequent burial at locations far removed from its source.

The reason this mechanism is ignored by evolutionary geologists is that a worldwide flood would imply extremely rapid deposition of the majority of sedimentary rock layer deposits. This, in turn, destroys the possibility of huge periods of time between the rock layer accumulations. Without large time periods for rock formation, the naturalistic support for gradual biological evolution also collapses. Thus slow and gradual transport of sand (even though it fits the actual evidence no better than believing that Mr. Sandman magically blew millions of cubic feet of sand to its current locations) is still the preferred explanation within evolutionary textbooks.

2. *Sand Transported Cross Country*, Andrew Snelling, Answers Magazine, Vol. 3 No. 4, Oct. 2008.

SKEPTIC'S CORNER

The Appalachian Mountains and the Navajo Sandstone deposits are supposedly of vastly different ages - separated by many millions of years. The only explanation evolutionary geologists have proposed for the movement of sand from one location to the other is some sort of river system which they claim could have transported the sand over many millions of years. Yet what river could sweep a specific type of sand to a specific location, while depositing no other type of sediment to that location, and also leaving none of that sand at locations in-between? Furthermore, this hypothetical river would have to continue for millions of years without changing course and also deposit this sand uniformly in a layer covering hundreds of thousands of miles in area and hundreds of feet in thickness. Mr. Sandman transporting the sand deposit sounds more plausible.

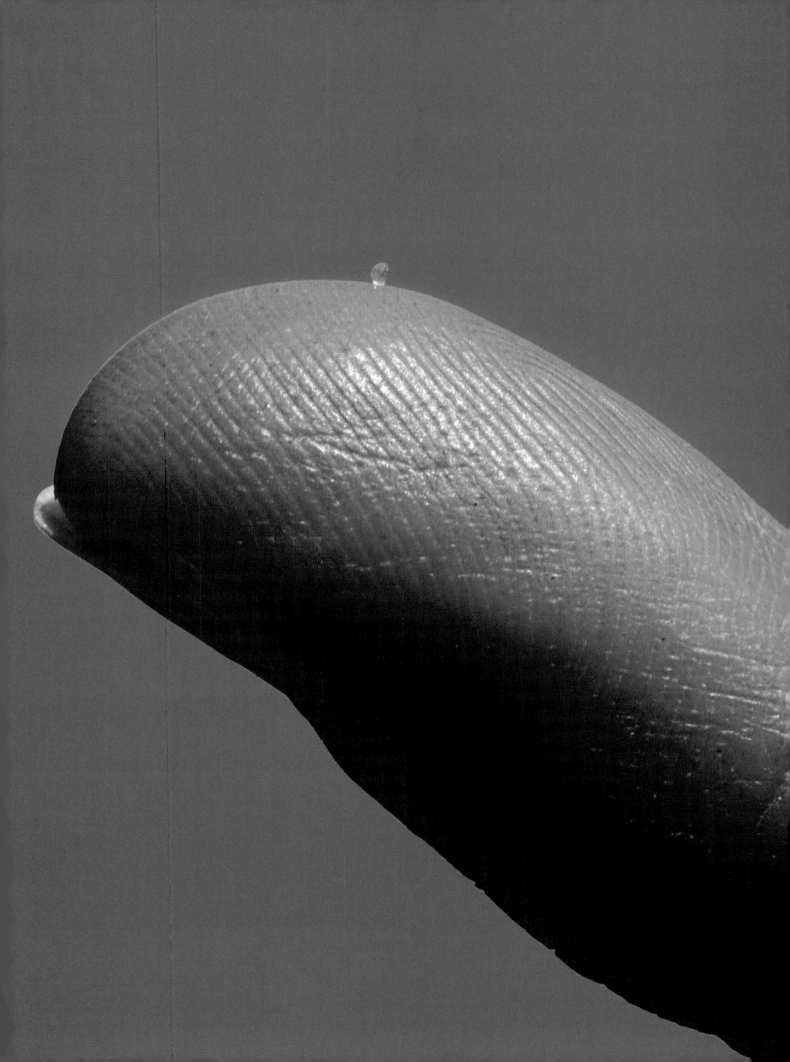

RIDICULED BUT RIGHT

Webster's dictionary defines a hero as, *"a person admired for his achievements"*, *"one who shows great courage"*, or *"the central figure in an event, period or movement"*. Because the human mind is built to filter everything through what it has been trained to believe is truth, it takes courageous and heroic men and women to propose ideas outside the accepted norm. These people are often discounted and ridiculed for presenting an idea contrary to the "majority consensus".

This is especially true in the area of science.

A perfect example is the work of geologist J. Harlan Bretz. In 1923, he published a paper which proposed the channeled Scablands (an eroded desert in Eastern Washington) were the result of an enormous flood in the distant past. Over the next forty years, Bretz published paper after paper supporting this idea. But his ideas were repeatedly opposed and ignored because they contradicted the evolutionary teaching of enormous periods and slow gradual changes.

Due primarily to Bretz' tenacity and heroic bravery in the face of opposition, all geologists today acknowledge that a catastrophic release of flowing water, not slow gradual erosional processes, carved out not just the Scablands of Washington, but much of Western Montana, Idaho, Washington and Oregon. This event has come to be known as the "Missoula Flood".

Near the end of the ice age (approximately 3600 years ago), a glacier blocked the Clark Fork River, filling a valley with 3000 feet of ice and damming up 540 cubic MILES of water to form a 2000-foot-deep lake near Missoula, Montana. At some point, the water broke through carrying icebergs the size of small towns all the way through Western Washington to the Pacific Ocean. While it is estimated that the lake took two days to drain, the flow rate from this single lake was ten times greater in volume than the combined flow rates of every river on Earth, creating a wall of water moving at 65 miles per hour. It is believed that just the roar from the moving water could be detected 30 miles ahead of the approaching catastrophe. Everything in its path was destroyed and in the process, the landscape of a large portion of Washington State was almost instantly transformed.[1,2,3] During this flood event:

SKEPTIC'S CORNER

Despite evidence such as the Missoula Flood's ability to rapidly transform enormous areas of landscape, it is still widely denied that the Earth ever experienced a world restructuring flood. The effects of Noah's Flood would have dwarfed the Missoula disaster, and both the Ice Age and the Missoula Flood were simply aftermaths of this global flood-reshaping catastrophe. Comparing the global flood to the Missoula Flood is like comparing a bucket of water poured onto an ocean beach to a six-foot pounding wave coming ashore. Today it is creation geologists who point to evidence for a world-restructuring flood (which is every bit as strong as the evidence for the Missoula Flood), and are opposed, rebuffed, and ignored.

- An estimated 200 feet depth of sediment was stripped from 16,000 square miles of the Scablands - cutting deep channels into volcanic bedrock and resulting in an enormous area of bare desert.
- Boulders as large as 30 feet and weighing half a million pounds were moved hundreds of miles.
- In some places, the width of the flow was 100 miles across – narrowing downstream to carve out the Grand Coulee River Valley, the Columbia River Valley, and then leave a 300-foot-deep channel carved off the coast of Washington, now located underwater at the edge of the continental shelf.
- Enormous waterfalls destroyed the landscape – some of them 3 ½ miles wide and 400 feet tall – gouging sheer cliffs into the surrounding valley.

In spite of the extensive evidence supporting the power of moving water to transform a landscape, it was not until the 1960s and availability of high altitude photographs that J. Harlan Bretz was totally vindicated. Despite acknowledging the Missoula Flood, evolutionary geologists have to believe there were dozens of floods in the area over a 100,000 year period of Earth history. Without the long time periods, a recent creation and worldwide flood triggering the ice age are the only other option. Just as they ridiculed Bretz almost a century ago, today evolutionists ridicule anyone who would challenge this old timeframe.

1. Official Park Service video from Dry Falls State Park, WA, 2008.
2. *Gigaflood: The Lake Missoula Flood in NW Oregon, & SW Washington,* Rick Thompson, DSA, 2014.
3. *Creation Explorers: Tracking the Flood,* Pike Pictures, www.creationexplorers.com, 2014.

CENSORED COSMOLOGY

Light takes billions of years to travel from the edge of the universe to earth. Thus it is assumed that the universe must be billions of years old, or we would not see the light which left these stars billions of years ago. A universe which is billions of earth-years old is foundational to the story of evolution. This idea is seldom questioned by professors, students or the media. Yet the Bible asserts that all of the heavens and everything upon the earth was created recently in six ordinary days less than 10,000 years ago. How can the two possibilities be reconciled?

Like mortar dropping from between the blocks of a weakening structure, the evidence is mounting that the story of cosmic evolution (requiring huge periods of time) has serious problems which are being suppressed, rather than examined. To openly admit to the contradictions and major flaws in the big bang theory of cosmic evolution casts too much doubt upon the naturalistic basis on which the "third rope" of humanistic thought depends. Thus the evidence supporting the recent creation of the universe and any problems with the naturalistic explaination of star, galaxy, and the universe formation are simply swept under the proverbial rug and suppressed.

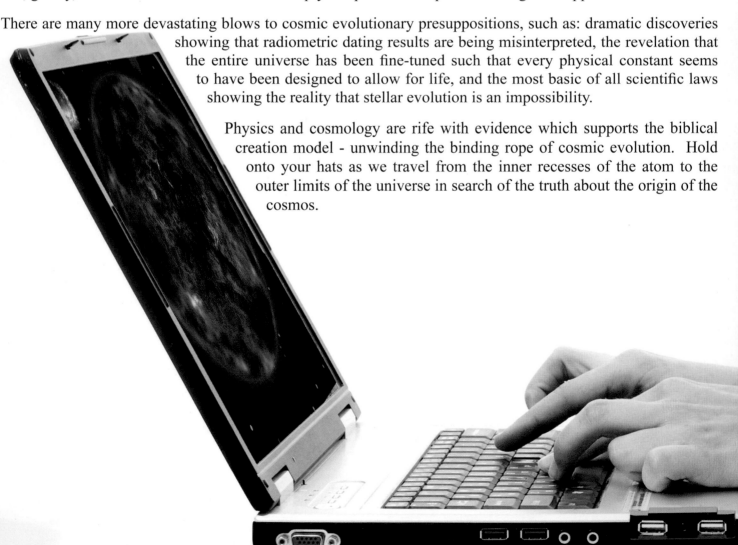

There are many more devastating blows to cosmic evolutionary presuppositions, such as: dramatic discoveries showing that radiometric dating results are being misinterpreted, the revelation that the entire universe has been fine-tuned such that every physical constant seems to have been designed to allow for life, and the most basic of all scientific laws showing the reality that stellar evolution is an impossibility.

Physics and cosmology are rife with evidence which supports the biblical creation model - unwinding the binding rope of cosmic evolution. Hold onto your hats as we travel from the inner recesses of the atom to the outer limits of the universe in search of the truth about the origin of the cosmos.

Cosmological Naturalism

Sometimes silence reveals truth better than a symphony of sound. For almost fifty years, we have been searching the skies for signs of intelligent communication from another planet. Surely there must be other intelligent forms of life amongst stars more numerous than all the leaves on all the plants on earth. We have looked in every "nook and cranny" of the universe, scanned every slice of the electromagnetic spectrum, and searched round the clock for any peep from little green men. Yet not a sentence, not a word, not an intelligible sound has been forthcoming.

The earth is located in a perfect location for observing the rest of the universe - near the very center - so that we are able to observe the rest of the heavens in every direction. We are between spiral arms near the outside edge of our own galaxy so that our view is not obscured by numerous other stars. Is this perfect position for both life to exist and the observation of the rest of the universe mere chance?

Our moon is exactly 1/400th the diameter of the sun and located exactly 1/400th of the distance from the earth to the sun. This enables perfect solar eclipses so that we are able to measure and understand the composition of the sun. Were the moon even slightly smaller or larger, even slightly closer or farther, we would know relatively little about stellar composition. Many discoveries have been aided by solar eclipses and no other moon/planet interaction comes close to this perfect balance. Could earth's be a product of random arrangement?

The earth is exactly the right distance from the sun to allow life to exist. If the sun were even slightly closer or farther the earth would become a steam bath or an ice planet with perpetually clouded skies. Our magnetic field is also perfectly balanced to keep solar radiation from stripping away our thin atmosphere, which shields us from harmful radiation. Could all of this be caused by a roll of the "cosmic dice"?

Even the basic physical constants of the universe seem perfectly balanced to allow life. If gravity, nuclear forces holding atoms together, the speed of light, the charge of electrons, or a host of other fundamental variables of the universe changed even minutely life would be impossible. How did our universe just happen to form with such finely tuned constants and laws of physics which seem to be designed with a knife-edge balance to hold it all together? [1]

Hundreds of factors are needed to maintain life anyplace within our universe, and each of these factors can be estimated by its probability of occurring at random. If any of these factors fell outside of a small range, life could not develop. The probability of all the needed conditions occurring on a given planet is a multiplication of all the factors – like the odds of dice rolling "double sixes" a trillion times in a row. Yet our planet is so perfectly tuned for life, and for the observation of the rest of the universe, that it is less likely to exist than rolling a pair of dice for every subatomic particle within the entire universe, for every second of the assumed fifteen billion-year age of the universe and every single roll coming up double sixes. Obviously, something other than chance is at work.

The deafening silence coming from every corner of the universe screams in silent testimony that what God has created on earth, including us, is incredibly special. Moreover, He has given us an impossibly privileged position to observe all that He made throughout the cosmos - in order that we could not possibly miss His power, majesty, and painstaking attention to every detail of creation.

1. *The Privileged Planet: How Our Place in the Cosmos is Designed for Discovery*, Guillermo Gonzalez & Jay Richards, Regnery Publishing, 2004.

SKEPTIC'S CORNER

Naturalists, atheists, and evolutionists have faith that all of the finely balanced conditions, perfect for life on earth, happened by chance. They have faith that earth could not possibly be unique in the vastness of the cosmos, so other forms of life must have developed out there someplace. They have enough faith to invest billions (much of it our tax dollars) in the search for that alien life. They continue to have faith even after fifty years of non-stop searching with nothing but silence to show for the investment of time and money. Isn't it infinitely more reasonable to believe that the finely tuned design of our planet, perfectly positioned and designed for both life and observation of the universe, is the gift of our Creator?

In The Beginning was the Word

Language can be expressed in an enormous number of ways. Verbal language is a series of sound waves traveling in recognized patterns through the air. But how can a language be differentiated from random noise or simple patterns?

There are over 6,000 different languages on earth, commonly divided into approximately thirty very distinct and essentially unrelated language groups. Intelligently generated language is used to express, preserve and communicate thoughts, information and abstract concepts. The vehicle for communicating language can be produced by codes as simple as a zero/one (binary) or a dot/dash/space (Morse code) or as complicated as ancient Chinese symbols (using 50,000 distinctly different characters). These codes can be written on paper, transmitted through the air via radio, television, or light waves, stored as electrons on a computer chip, or saved as an arrangement of physical objects as simple as rocks arranged on a beach. Yet it is only an intelligent form of communication if there is a receiver capable of decoding the information for a purpose. The medium through which a message is recorded is irrelevant in determining whether the communication comes from an intelligent source.

There are several distinct requirements for determining if any form of communication comes from an intelligent origin meant to convey detailed information rather than artwork or random noise. Suppose you came across a set of symbols on a cave wall or a set of rocks arranged on a beach. How could you determine if it was communication, art, or a chance arrangement? First, the symbols have to be in a non-repeated pattern. If the symbols simply repeat over and over, very little, if any, information can be communicated. Second, the symbols must be reused in some sequence. If no symbol is repeated, essentially nothing can be communicated. This first level of complexity for a language can be measured by simple statistics. But this is only the first step toward communication. Even spilling a set of Scrabble letters can result in some intelligible words.

It is only the pre-determined (and agreed upon) arrangement into specific orders and spaces which can communicate large and complex concepts. This is called syntax. The letters, spaces, and punctuation upon this page demonstrate this. Yet the language is still largely useless unless three more things are present: The communicated language must be understood by something receiving the message (semantics), the message must implement an action (pragmatics), and a useful result must happen (apobetics). If any arrangement of electromagnetic or physical objects fulfill all five of these criteria, it is an absolute certainty that communication from an intelligent source has occurred.

The code upon the DNA molecule fulfills every one of these requirements for the definition of communication from an intelligent origin. DNA is made by the complex repetition of four chemicals in a specific, designated order. This results in other chemicals receiving and replicating this sequence upon other molecules, which results in the implementation of actions with a useful purpose. Every requirement of useful communication, on a level far surpassing current human understanding, is present.[1]

We are just now learning to decode and understand the purpose of the communication written upon this molecule. There can be no realistic doubt that the DNA code is, indeed, a result of intelligent design. Even the three billion letters in the human genome do not adequately explain all of the complexity of the human body. Leaders in the field of genetics are now speculating that, in addition to carrying information in a linear fashion (like letters in a sentence), the DNA molecule also carries information in a three-dimensional fashion. This would be analogous to letters on page 12 of this book interacting with letters on page 88 to carry additional communication to a reader.

We are like babies trying to understand the mind of Einstein in our current ability to fully understand the DNA molecule and living cells. Yet our schools, blinded by an assumption of naturalism, acknowledge the code but fail to recognize the code-maker.

SKEPTIC'S ? CORNER

Evolutionists will deny to their last breath that
the coded information upon the DNA molecule
is intelligently generated communication. If
they were to do otherwise, they would cease
to be evolutionists. Yet this denial is based on
faith that flies in the face of the actual evidence.
There is no realistic definition for intelligent
communication, when applied to the coding in
the DNA molecule, that does not clearly show
that its origin is an intelligent designer.

Star Evolution

The number of stars in the universe is of approximately the same magnitude as the total number of sand grains covering every beach on earth. The universe contains about one hundred billion galaxies, each containing an average of one hundred billion stars. One of the many problems with the big bang model is the reality that spiral-shaped galaxies should not still exist if they had formed at the beginning of the big bang expansion fifteen billion years ago. This is because spiral-shaped galaxies have stars at the outside edges rotating around an axis more slowly than the stars near the center. Because the stars are rotating within the galaxies at different speeds, if these galaxies had formed billions of years ago, the distinct spiral shape would long ago have disappeared. Cosmologists attempting to explain the formation of the universe (without accepting the idea of its recent formation by God) are forced to believe that stars have been continuously forming throughout history in order to account for the relatively young appearance of these common spiral galaxies. They postulate that most of the new stars form in spiral-shaped zones.

This is the problem: for 100,000,000,000 galaxies times 100,000,000,000 stars to have formed within the assumed age of the universe (13,800,000,000 years), an average of twenty thousand new stars would have to have formed during each second of those 13.8 billion years.

Astronomers have directly and indirectly witnessed the destruction of thousands of stars. These exploding stars are called supernovas. **Yet, there is not a single documented, undisputed case of a new star forming - anywhere in the known universe.** No one has ever shown a photograph of any part of the universe compared with an earlier photograph of that same portion of the sky with a new star appearing within the photographic image. To account for all of the stars in the universe, twenty thousand new stars should be appearing every second.

Scientists cannot even explain how a star could form. Stars are enormous, densely packed spheres of hydrogen gas with nuclear fusion taking place inside, resulting in the release of enormous amounts of energy. Yet hydrogen gas will not condense into a super-concentrated ball within the vacuum of space for three fundamental reasons: First, gas gets hotter as the molecules are forced closer and closer together. Long before gravity could become strong enough to take over and condense nebular hydrogen clouds, the gas pressure would be a million times too strong to allow the continued collapse of the cloud. Second, the gas

SKEPTIC'S CORNER

Skeptics assume stars are still forming by natural processes because the only alternative is that God supernaturally produced them relatively recently. There have been many speculative mechanisms proposed to explain star formation. Popular theories include the idea that supernovas produce shock waves or that spiral density waves exist, either of which could condense nebular gas clouds into new stars. Three problems are essentially ignored:

1. From where did the first generation stars come … to form the supernovas … to form the new stars?

2. Why would shock waves or spiral density waves force material together to form a star, rather than spreading out the gas?

3. "Spiral density waves" are mathematical story-telling; they have never been observed nor their origin explained.

Using such speculation to explain star formation is like explaining the existence of a sand castle by a "castle-forming wave" coming across a beach and forming an exquisite castle in its wake.

within the nebular clouds is rotating. As the material is pulled closer, it would rotate faster and the increasing angular momentum would drive the material apart, not allowing it to condense into a star. Third, nebular gas fields have a magnetic field associated with them. As the material within this field collapses, the field would become increasingly concentrated and the material would repel like the poles of two magnets. Thus, there is no mechanism explaining the formation of stars, while there are numerous observations indicating that stars cannot form by any natural process.[1]

Sir Arthur Conan Doyle lived at the time of Darwin and was no friend of the Bible. Yet his imaginative mind created the most famous detective in literature - Sherlock Holmes. This master of reason observed, *"When you have eliminated the impossible, whatever remains, however improbable, must be the truth."*[2] The natural gas laws, magnetic force laws, and angular momentum laws all preclude the possibility that hydrogen gas could condense to form a star – and we have never observed even a single star form. All known natural explanations for the formation of stars have impossible obstacles, leaving the improbable, yet possible, explanation that stars exist simply as stated in Genesis 1:16 because "[God] made the stars also." How sad that this is the one possibility that is never allowed to be seriously considered by students in our universities and school systems.

1. *Taking Back Astronomy*, Dr. Jason Lisle, Master Books, 2006.
2. *The Sign of the Four*, Sir Arthur Conan Doyle, Mystery Author and Physician, 1859 – 1930.

Ancient Tombs and Helium Balloons

I have saved my money for many years so that I could take a trip to the Holy Land. Upon arriving at my hotel I am greeted in the lobby by a man who informs me that only yesterday he and his brother found the entrance to an ancient tomb likely to contain great treasures and artifacts at least two thousand years old. According to Abdul, this excavation was in an area of Israel never explored by others. For a mere five hundred dollars he would allow me, an illustrious visitor to his land, to be the first person ever to open the door and explore the chamber therein. Being a trusting person, I gladly pay Abdul for such an opportunity, and we set off into the desert.

Sure enough, it is a long and arduous journey through paths and hills which exhibit no signs of civilization. We travel through a barely visible crack in a canyon wall and come to an ancient carving in front of a tunnel of obvious human origin. After lighting lanterns, we push ahead brushing aside cobwebs covering the entrance; we walk, crawl, and squeeze through the dusty passageways.

Finally, we come to the promised sealed doorway to unknown treasure. As agreed, Abdul lets me be the first person, in over two thousand years, to open the door and walk into the mysterious chamber. As I peer into the room of obvious ancient origin, I first see the dust-covered, uneven, hand-hewn blocks of stone. The tomb entrance is lit by openings to the sky, allowing light to filter down from above. I believe I am the first to look upon this scene in over two thousand years - until I look up and see numerous helium balloons floating on the ceiling. That's when I know I've been fleeced. The fact that the helium balloons are still floating proves that thousands of years had not passed and that someone else had recently been escorted to the "ancient" tomb.

Radiometric dating methods are commonly used to "prove" that the earth is billions of years old. There are inconsistencies in these methods, but overall, radiometric dating provides a compelling and consistent picture that at today's rate of decay, billions of years worth of radioactive decay has happened to dozens of different radioactive isotopes found in the rock layers of our planet. Radiometric dating methods are based on the measurement of decayed materials within rock samples. It is analogous to looking at the amount of sand in the bottom of an hour glass. By knowing the rate at which the sand moves from the top to the bottom, you can calculate how much time has passed.

The Bible states that "in six days God made the heavens and the earth" (Exodus 20:11) and that this event happened quite recently (Genesis 5). Therefore, either the Bible does not mean what it clearly and repeatedly states, or there is something wrong with the assumptions of radiometric dating methods. For over one hundred years a majority of theologians have been laboring to explain why the Bible must not mean what it says. This has had predictable results – the deterioration of people's trust in God's Word. Recent discoveries by scientists, however, have uncovered astounding and revolutionary evidence which sheds completely new light on this century-old controversy.[1]

Many radioactive decay processes spew out an alpha particle, which rapidly turns into a helium atom. The decay of uranium^{238} to lead^{206} actually involves eight transformations, resulting in eight new atoms of helium for every atom of decayed uranium. Since much of the uranium in the earth's crust is concentrated as an impurity inside zircon crystals, this helium starts out trapped inside these zircon crystals in granitic rocks. Until a few years ago no one had measured the migration (leakage) rate of helium out of zircon.

Helium is a very small, energetic atom which will migrate at a measurable rate through any substance at a constant rate. This is why even aluminized helium balloons do not remain floating indefinitely. By measuring the amount of helium which formed, the amount remaining in the crystal, and the rate at which it leaks out, the time when the radioactive decay occurred can be accurately determined. This has now been done for multiple granite formations, at different depths, and taking temperature into account. The result of the most recent experiments is the astonishing conclusion that the radioactive decay which created the helium (thought to have occurred billions of years ago) actually took place within the last six thousand years, give or take a few hundred years. The helium could not possibly still be trapped in trillions of these tiny zircon crystals around the planet if those rock formations are actually millions of years old.

God has left trillions of microscopic "helium balloons" (zircon crystals within granite formations) that still contain helium - helium that could not possibly be there if these crystals had formed more than a few thousand years ago. So does this indicate that granite is younger than commonly thought? What are the implications for earth history if granite is young? This is just one of a multiplicity of evidences supporting the recent creation of our planet. There are many other data points like this which strongly indicate the need for a more open discussion of the age of the earth. The reason these types of discoveries are never acknowledged in schools and museums is because the "tour guides" of modern naturalistic science require an enormously old earth in order to maintain their belief that life arose on its own without God.

1. *Thousands Not Billions: Challenging an Icon of Evolution*, Don DeYoung, Master Books, 2005.

SKEPTIC'S CORNER

The amazing discovery of the helium still present in these zircon crystals is more than five years old. The response from "old age" skeptics include such possibilities as - temperature was not taken into account, "something" kept the helium in, the helium migrated in from other sources, and the measurements were done in a lab, whereas rocks are in the field.

These responses simply do not explain away the evidence. Temperature was taken into account, other major minerals in granite have a higher (not lower) leakage rate than the zircon within which the helium is found, helium could no more concentrate itself within the crystals than it could randomly flow into a metalized balloon to keep it floating, and the higher pressures within the granite formation where the samples were obtained have a negligible effect on the density of the zircon relative to the conditions in the lab.

What this evidence has generated most is silence - because the evidence is so strong. The primary strategy of those conditioned to believe in an old age paradigm is simply to ignore these astonishing findings.

Einstein and the Oort Cloud

Early in the twentieth century the scientific community taught that the universe was essentially eternal. As the vast size of the universe became apparent, it was commonly believed that the universe was neither expanding nor contracting because both would imply an origin for the universe which included the undesirable philosophical baggage of an Originator.

While Einstein was working on his general theory of relativity, his mathematical equations clearly indicated that the universe ought to be either contracting or expanding due to gravitational forces. Yet Einstein so strongly believed in a static universe (not because of observation but because of naturalistic preconceptions) that he added a "cosmological constant" (a fudge factor) to his general theory of relativity in order to balance the force of gravity and maintain the dogma of a static universe. He did this because, if the universe is eternal and static, no origin and no creator are required to account for its existence.

It was only after understanding the observations of Edwin Hubble (that the universe was indeed expanding) that Einstein realized his mistake. To his credit, Einstein dropped the factor from his equations and acknowledged this error. Yet a similar situation exists today.

One of the most fascinating features of our solar system is the periodic appearance of comets as they circle the sun. In ancient times, the appearance of comets was considered an evil omen, with great fear and panic accompanying their appearance. We now know that these heavenly bodies are relatively small (one to thirty miles in diameter) balls of dirty ice circling the sun from far out in the solar system. The characteristic tail of the comet is due to the sun melting part of the ice ball and sending a cloud of dust particles and ionized gas trailing for millions of miles behind the comet as it circles close to the sun. With each trip around the sun, the comet loses some of its material and the "snowball" becomes smaller.

It is easy to calculate the longevity of known comets; the vast majority of comets could not possibly have been around for more than 10,000 years. The large number of comets still present today is direct observational evidence that the solar system is quite young. This observation is inconvenient baggage to the philosophical belief that the solar system evolved long ago rather than that it was created quite recently. In order to explain the presence of abundant comets still present within our solar system, Dutch astronomer Jan Hendrik Oort proposed that there was a depository containing billions of new comets outside of our solar system which occasionally kicked new comets into orbit around our sun.

This "solution" to the dilemma of how these comets could still exist if the solar system were billions of years old has become a dogmatic belief taught within astronomy; however, this cloud of ice balls has never been observed, nor have any new comets originating from it been identified. In essence, what Oort did was add an unobserved fudge factor to explain the existence of comets within the dogma of a billion-year-old solar system. This fudge factor of modern astronomy is no different in concept than Einstein's erroneous "cosmological constant." Both errors are examples of efforts to explain away the obvious in order to maintain a naturalistic belief in creation without a Creator.

SKEPTIC'S CORNER

Evolution, whether cosmic, chemical, geological, or biological, needs huge periods of time to make it credible. Thus any observation which indicates recent origin - such as the relatively short life of comets - is ignored. Meanwhile, speculative explanations - such as the existence of an unseen Oort cloud - are taught as fact. Even the late Carl Sagan (who was instrumental in popularizing cosmic evolution during the latter part of the twentieth century) admitted in his book *Comet*, "Many scientific papers are written each year about the Oort cloud, its properties, its origin, its evolution. Yet there is not a shred of direct observational evidence for its existence."

Our universe has been personified as an ancient grandfather whose age is beyond comprehension. One of the primary reasons for this belief is the time it would take for light from the outer edges of the universe to reach the earth. Light travels approximately 186,000 miles per second, so photons leaving the surface of the sun require about eight minutes to reach the earth. Light leaving other stars takes much longer. It takes 4.3 years for light from the closest star to reach the earth and approximately 60,000 years for starlight from the far edge of our own galaxy to reach earth. Light from stars at the farthest edge of the universe would take approximately 14 billion years to traverse the heavens. If the stars in the universe were created only 6,000 earth years ago (as the Bible indicates), how could light from the most remote stars have reached earth?

The key to the age-old conundrum of how starlight from distant stars could have reached the earth if the entire universe had been created only 6,000 years ago (from an earth vantage point) can be found using many verses from Scripture which describe the stretching out of the heavens. There are at least seventeen different Bible verses which describe God's method of forming the cosmos by stretching it out. For example, Job 9:8 says, "He alone spreads out the heavens," and Psalm 104:2 states that "... [He who] stretches out the heavens like a curtain." These statements have enormous implications for astrophysics.

Modern physics has discovered a number of mind-boggling observations concerning the nature of time, space, and matter:

• Time is part of the physical universe, and the rate at which it changes is dependent on the mass, acceleration, and speed of anything in the vicinity of the measurement.

• Space itself is not "nothing" but "something" which can be bent and stretched and which seems to consist of an enormous amount of energy.

• Mass can be transformed into energy but cannot be accelerated faster than the speed of light because the faster mass is accelerated, the "heavier" it becomes, and the more energy is required to accelerate it further. Thus infinite speed would require infinite energy.

As far as we know, nothing with mass can be accelerated faster than the speed of light. Thus distant stars seem to imply a very ancient cosmos. Given these observations, there are at least three explanations for how distant starlight could have reached earth in a recent creation:

For one, the speed of light may have been exceedingly faster during the creation of the universe; however, this is mostly speculation, with unconfirmed experimental or observational support.

Second, time itself may have elapsed at different speeds in different locations during the stretching out of the cosmos. Many observations also place the earth near the center of the known universe. If one folds this observation into Einstein's equations of relativity and expand the entire mass of the universe outward, one finds that billions of years elapse in the outer reaches of the universe while only days were passing in the vicinity of the earth. Thus light from these stars would have had billions of "star years" to reach the earth in mere "earth days." [1]

Finally, God may have expanded space itself during the formation of the universe. This would not have been noticeable while it was happening because any physical "yardstick" for measuring distance would have been expanding at the same time as the distances were expanding. The rate at which this expansion could take place would not be limited by the speed of light because space has no mass. Therefore, the universe could have been expanded at billions of times the speed of light. If the stars were formed within a relatively small universe as the universe was expanding, light would have rapidly reached the earth and the subsequent continued expansion of space itself would explain the current size of the universe. This would also explain the background radiation present throughout the universe and the red shift of light coming from distant galaxies - all within a six-day time frame from the perspective of a planet located near the mass center of the universe, i.e. the earth.[2]

God is making it increasingly apparent that His Word is to be understood in a clear, straightforward way. There really is no scientific justification for rejecting the straightforward biblical understanding that the universe was, indeed, created in six literal, normal, twenty-four hour earth days. Grandfather Time might not be quite so old after all.

1. *Starlight and Time: Solving the Puzzle of Distant Starlight in a Young Universe*, D. Russell Humphreys, Master Books, 1994.

2. *Starlight, Time, and the New Physics*, John Hartnett, Creation Book Publishers, 2007.

SKEPTIC'S CORNER

The Big Bang model for the formation of the universe, with its required billions of years of earth history, is actually fraught with significant problems; however, since there is currently no better naturalistic model, the majority of the astronomers trained in naturalism continue to cling to big bang cosmology. Either Dr. Russell Humphreys' "white hole cosmology" or Dr. John Hartnett's "fifth dimensional space expansion" model explains the data much better; however, both explanations place the earth in a unique location within the universe (near the center), and when the mathematical implications are properly understood, both result in an unacceptably young age for the earth. Thus both models are rejected by naturalistic cosmologists in spite of the fact that they explain the formation of the universe better than the Big Bang model.

SKEPTIC'S CORNER

Belief in the formation of the universe without God requires huge periods of time and therefore requires the belief in some sort of regenerating magnetic field; yet all of the planets have decaying magnetic fields which "coincidentally" match the decay rate predicted by their size and properties if they were created *"out of water and by means of water"* approximately 6,000 years ago.

The test which divides science from storytelling is the ability to predict the results of experiments and guide future discoveries. The origin of the planets provides such a test by allowing us to determine whether recent creation or slow evolution best explains their planets' measured magnetic fields.

A magnetic field is the result of the alignment of a charge along an axis. In a rectangular bar magnet, the magnetism results from the atoms of iron being aligned in one direction - allowing the spin of the charged electrons to create magnetic lines of force, flowing from one pole to the other. These lines of magnetic force can be passed from one conductive material to another - aligning the magnetic forces in the new material. Entire planets, stars, and even galaxies can become "magnetized" with a measurable magnetic strength (called the "magnetic flux"). Without this magnetic field, the earth would be uninhabitable because the field deflects a significant portion of the high-energy-charged radiation coming from the sun. Without this field, our thin layer of atmospheric gases could be stripped away and life on earth would be exposed to much higher levels of lethal radiation. The questions which science must answer are, "From where did this magnetic flux come and how long has it existed?"

There are only two possible explanations for planetary magnetic fields. Either they are continuously regenerated by some sort of internal dynamo (generator mechanism) within the core of the planets or they were created when the planets were formed and have been decaying ever since.

In 1984, long before the magnetic fields of the outer planets were measured, Dr. Russell Humphreys predicted the magnetic flux strength of all major planetary bodies. He made this prediction based on the assumption that God's Word was written with a straightforward meaning and that 2 Peter 3:5 could be understood to say, "*[B]y the word of God, the heavens and the earth of old were formed out of water and by means of water.*" If this is meant to be understood in a straightforward way, then it means that God started with water and transformed this material into all of the other elements as He expanded the universe. Thus the magnetic flux within enormous amounts of aligned dipolar water molecules would be passed on to the planets, stars, and even galaxies during the subsequent transformation and expansion. By knowing the time at which the creation happened (approximately 6,000 years ago) and knowing the mass and composition of the various heavenly bodies, it is straightforward mathematics to calculate the decay rates of the magnetic fields of the planets and thereby predict their current strengths, even before it is actually measured.

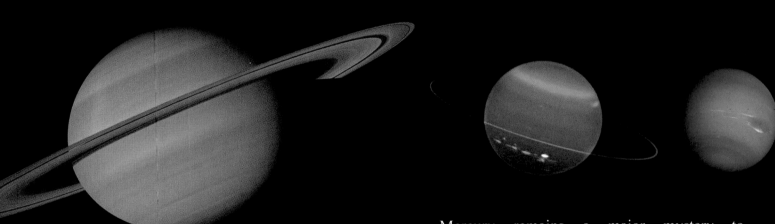

Mercury remains a major mystery to evolutionists because its small size should have allowed its core to solidify (if it is billions of years old). A solid core could have no dynamo to regenerate a planet's magnetic field so if the dynamo theory is correct, no magnetic field should be present on Mercury. Yet, it has been found to have a magnetic flux of almost exactly the strength which Dr. Humphreys' recent creation theory predicted, and the field is decaying as would be expected if the planet were formed a mere 6,000 years ago. The dynamo theory was also wrong about the field strength and alignment on Uranus, Neptune, and many other planets and moons within our solar system, whereas the recent creation from water predictions were right on - long before Mariner 10 in 1975 found that the magnetic field existed on these planets. These field strengths and alignments were subsequently measured in January 2008 by Messenger space probes.

The Humphreys model, which starts from a straightforward understanding of Scripture, even correctly predicted the magnetic force lines found within spiral galaxies, stars, and the entire universe.[1] It would seem that, once again, taking Scripture at face value supports scientific discovery, whereas assuming God's Word does not mean what it states in a clear, straightforward way hinders the advancement of science.

1. *The Creation of Cosmic Magnetic Fields*, D. Russell Humphreys, Proceedings of the Sixth International Conference on Creationism (pp.213-230), 2009.

Diamonds and Hot Coal

Imagine sitting with a group of friends and having only one donut to share. You break the donut in half and pass what's left to the next person. Each person breaks the donut in half, giving the next person the remainder. Each person down the line receives half as much as the person before – $\frac{1}{2}$, $\frac{1}{4}$, $\frac{1}{8}$, $\frac{1}{16}$, $\frac{1}{32}$, $\frac{1}{64}$, $\frac{1}{128}$, $\frac{1}{256}$, $\frac{1}{512}$, $\frac{1}{1024}$, etc… By the tenth person there isn't even a crumb left. Radiocarbon dating works the same way.

Diamonds and coal are both made of carbon. Slow and gradual coal formation is always presented as a fact in science books and museums. Students are shown pictures of ancient swamps filled with extinct creatures and told that during the "Carboniferous period" of earth's history (supposedly 30 – 360 million years ago) swamps covered the landscape and dead organic matter slowly turned to coal.[1] We are also told that the age of diamonds dwarf even these vast time passages – diamonds supposedly formed deep within the Earth 2-4 billion years ago.[2] Yet carbon-14 (^{14}C) dating reveals that neither coal nor diamonds could be this old.

It has recently been discovered that both coal and diamonds contain measurable amounts of radiocarbon.[3] Carbon-14 dating has long been heralded as the definitive proof that the Bible is wrong when it speaks of a 6,000-year-old Earth. Carbon-14 is a radioactive element present in all living organisms which disappears over time as the unstable carbon isotope decays to form other elements. At today's decay rate, one half of any original ^{14}C disappears every 5,730 years.

As long as any organism is alive, it is taking in radioactive carbon and making every cell of its body using this radioactive carbon. However, as soon as it dies, the radiocarbon starts to decay, and within 5,730 years half of the original material disappears. In approximately 12,000 years three-quarters of the original ^{14}C is gone. In about 18,000 years ninety percent is gone. Since the original amount of ^{14}C in living organisms is incredibly small, the ^{14}C level rapidly reaches an immeasurable amount. At the current decay rate of radioactive carbon, this corresponds to cutting the original level in half approximately eighteen times (this would happen in less than 100,000 years). Carbon-14 decays so fast that not a single atom of ^{14}C could remain in only 250,000 years. Thus, if ^{14}C is found in coal or diamonds, it is definitive proof that these substances cannot be millions of years old.

It is a scientific fact that every known coal seam contains an average 0.25% of modern radiocarbon levels.[3] This is 250 times greater than the detection limit of the analytical equipment. A single molecule should not be left if coal were deposited millions of years ago! How do the radiocarbon experts explain all this extra radiocarbon? They simply label it "background contamination", limit the method to an accuracy of "50,000 years", and ignore the problem and implications. Even diamonds, which are the hardest natural substance and could not have been infiltrated with modern carbon contamination, can be ground up and shown to contain hundreds of times too much radioactive carbon. The evidence from modern science confirms that coal and diamonds could not have formed billions of years ago.

It is readily apparent from the carbon-14 remaining in both coal and diamonds that the Earth formed quite recently. Let's return to our donut analogy. Since there is still a significant portion of "the donut" left, there could not have been millions of people in line cutting it in half. God is making it undeniably apparent in our lifetime that the Bible is meant to be understood in a clear straightforward way. Creation was a recent event.

1. http://www.wsgs.uwyo.edu/coalweb/default.aspx
2. http://www.amnh.org/exhibitions/diamonds/
3. *Radioisotopes and the Age of the Earth: Results of a Young Earth Creationist Research Initiative*, Dr. Larry Vardiman, Master Books, 2005.

SKEPTIC'S CORNER

Finding ^{14}C atoms still present in coal and other buried sediments is incompatible with the evolutionary mindset, so a decade-long effort to eliminate any possible source of modern carbon contamination was undertaken by the radiocarbon industry. They totally failed. The presence of extra radiocarbon is simply labeled as "background contamination" and subtracted from the result -- in spite of the fact that there is no explanation for how it could have gotten there. One proposed explanation for the presence of [14]C (which should not exist) is that modern bacteria eat the coal and bring in modern carbon. It is such suggestions which most clearly reveal the desperation of the evolutionary model. Bacteria living on coal would be using the old carbon (containing no ^{14}C) to make their cellular structure, so this does not account for the continued presence of modern ^{14}C in coal deposits where it simply should not exist.

SKEPTIC'S CORNER

What happened in the distant past cannot be repeated and ALL dating methods depend on unprovable assumptions. Unless we know the rate of change over the entire period of time being measured, as well as the starting amounts being measured, and have absolute proof that no form of contamination has occurred, no dating method provides proof for the age of the earth. Those looking for truth need to examine the quality of the data supporting creation and consider the validity of reasons for rejecting it. Are the rejections based on valid data or just excuses to cling to a belief in naturalism?

Greased Watermelons

One of the favorite swimming pool games at Boy Scout camps is known as the greased watermelon contest. The idea behind the game is to put two teams of boys into a swimming pool along with a watermelon which has been covered with grease - making it essentially impossible to grab. The team which succeeds in moving the watermelon to its end of the pool wins the game. The best strategy for winning is to conceal the watermelon below the surface of the water, hiding the truth of where it resides from the opposing team, while moving it forward. Yet the watermelon keeps popping up because it is simply too slippery to hold down. The truth about the age of the earth acts similarly.

Evolution absolutely requires a belief in enormous periods of time in order to make the upward transformation of life plausible. Thus, any dating method which seems to indicate a huge age for the earth is accepted, while any method that seems to indicate a young age for the earth is suppressed. But, just like the greased watermelon, no matter how hard they are submersed, young age indicators keep popping up. It is the breadth and depth of the young age indicators, popping up in all different disciplines of science, which form the convincing argument for our recent creation. For instance:

- Helium, formed by radioactive decay processes, is still present in trillions of zircon granite crystals, even though we know this gas would have escaped from these rocks if they were millions of years old. This indicates the rock layers of the earth formed thousands, not billions of years ago, and that there has been a recent period of rapid radiometric decay (page 100).

- Unbroken yet folded sedimentary layers and sandstone intrusion of lower rock layers up through cracks in overlying layers both testify to the sedimentary rock layers of the earth having been laid down rapidly and recently (pages 64, 74).

- The historical documentation of healthy marriages between close relations only 3,000 to 4,500 years ago, while this is not possible today, testifies to the rapid deterioration of the human genome and indicates humanity could not possibly have been around for a million years (page 36).

- Permanent random changes (mistakes) building up on the genome of every living organism can now be tracked. Greater than ninety-nine percent of these are invisible to natural selection and therefore cannot be removed; yet it can be proven that this random information is rapidly destroying the viability of all forms of life – limiting the maximum age for all life on earth to a very recent creation (page 18).

- Unfossilized tissue has been found inside of dinosaur bones. This contradicts everything we know about the laws of chemistry and physics unless the bones were buried thousands rather than millions of years ago. This undecayed tissue simply should not exist (page 86).

- Radiocarbon is still present in coal, unfossilized dinosaur bones and other carbon-containing artifacts thought to be hundreds of millions of years old. The measured level is 500 times above instrument detection limits. Yet every single atom of radioactive carbon-14 should have disappeared within 250,000 years of the organisms' demise (page 108).

- The continued existence of spiraled galaxies and comets, the ability of light to reach the earth from the outer edges of the universe within days of creation, and the rapidly decaying magnetic field of the planets all testify to a recently created universe. (pages 102, 104, 106, 116)

These evidences for our recent creation are just the tip of the iceberg that keeps breaking through the surface of deception. When evidence is suppressed in one area, it just pops up in another area of science, such as carbon dating, or genetics, or history, or geology, or biology, or paleontology. One wonders how much longer the myth of an ancient earth can be maintained.

Bastard Stars

In small towns, gossip
is said to be the only thing exceeding
the speed of light. If a white couple gave birth to
a child with coal-black skin, it would be whispered that some
"hanky-panky" had been going on at the conception of the child. The
label of bastard[1] or illegitimate would follow the child as he grew up, based
on the evidence that his parents lacked some of the characteristics (black skin) which
the child possessed. It would be assumed that either his mother had broken her marriage
vows of faithfulness or one of the parents had a hidden African genetic heritage. There is a similar
relationship problem with stars - if the big bang model is true.

The big bang purports to explain the origin of all matter, including all of the stars and galaxies in the universe.
According to this theory, all of the energy of the universe was originally compressed into a small point of
singularity which explosively expanded, forming the first generation
of stars (known as "population III" stars). According to
physics, these stars would have consisted only
of hydrogen, helium, and trace amounts of
lithium.

To explain the presence of all the
other elements in the universe,
it is assumed that nuclear
transformations took place in
the core of these original stars,
and when these stars exploded the
heavier elements were redistributed
throughout the universe. From this first

SKEPTIC'S ? CORNER

Skeptics have faith that someday a natural explanation for the existence of stars will be found. They point out premature conclusions made by creationist scientists concerning the possibility that the sun's energy could not have been solely from nuclear fusion because early measurements indicated the sun was shrinking and there were missing neutrinos in the quantity expected by nuclear fusion. Subsequent evidence revealed that these conclusions were false and nuclear fusion does explain the energy of the sun. These claims are no longer made by reputable creation researchers.

There is a fundamental difference between speculation about the sun's operation and theories about the origin of the universe. In the case of a possible "shrinking sun" no one ever doubted that nuclear fusion was going on in the sun; evidence was just explored as to whether this was the sole mechanism generating the sun's power. In the case of missing generation III stars, not a single such star has ever been identified; yet there should be billions present throughout the galaxy if the big bang were correct. This indicates a fundamental flaw in the very fabric of the big bang model - leaving the skeptic with nothing but faith in naturalism to explain the origin of the universe.

generation of stars, the next generation of stars formed - but these stars were contaminated with trace amounts of the heavier elements (called "population II" stars). Finally, these stars exploded, and a third generation of stars formed with even higher concentrations of heavier elements ("population I" stars). Thus, stars with no heavy elements yielded stars with some heavy elements - which yielded stars with even more heavy elements. In other words, if the big bang theory is correct, each succeeding generation of stars (each with a lifetime of billions of years) would have characteristics completely unlike its parent - somewhat like illegitimate children. This story of star formation is interesting but, how can it be tested to see if the big bang is true?

All three of the different populations of stars have lifetimes estimated to be well in excess of the assumed 13.8 billion-year-age of the universe. Each year a tiny fraction of stars throughout the universe do explode in supernovas. But there are an estimated one hundred billion galaxies, each containing one hundred billion stars, so we would fully expect to find stars of all three population types throughout the universe. This is where "the plot thickens." In actuality, we only find second and third population stars - but ALL OF THEM are contaminated with heavy elements. None of these stars should have formed during the initial Big Bang expansion because the required first generation stars (without any heavier elements) are not present anywhere within the universe. It is as if the entire universe is filled with "bastard" stars and their parents (the stars made from only hydrogen, helium, and lithium) are nowhere to be found.[2]

The mysterious missing parent stars are an enormous unsolved problem for the big bang model. It simply cannot explain the appearance of actual stars in the universe. It is almost as if they were simply created throughout the universe, in enormous quantity and variety, in order to cause wonder and awe from intelligent observers.

1. The dictionary definition of "bastard" is a child born to a couple who are not married. There is no prohibition in the Bible for interracial marriage, and children resulting from interracial marriage will likely be quite varied in appearance and skin coloration. There is actually only one race – the human race – and the only biblical prohibition is sex outside of marriage or marriage of believers with non-believers.

2. *Dismantling the Big Bang: God's Universe Rediscovered*, Alex Williams, John Hartnett, Master Books, 2005.

Where'd all the mirrors Go?

My glove drawer irritates me. It is ninety percent right-hand gloves and ten percent left-hand gloves. Every time I go to look for garden gloves I need to hunt through the entire drawer to find a match. When purchased these gloves came in equal right-hand and left-hand quantities – identical in every way, but perfect mirror images of each other. It's like some gremlin sneaked in during the dark of the night and stole only the left-hand gloves. I refuse to get rid of the excess right-hand gloves because of a glimmer of hope that someday I'll find the depository of the missing mates.

Just like gloves, the universe around us is full of physical objects which can come in mirror images of each other. Yet we often find that the universe is composed of only one of the possible mirror images. Just as gloves are obviously manufactured by an intelligent designer, so the matter in the universe has been created and arranged in specific ways by an intelligent Creator. It is those missing mirror images which strongly point us toward that conclusion. Two examples are the molecules of life and the structure of matter.

The most common type of organic molecules are proteins. Our blood, hair, fingernails, ligaments, skin, muscles, etc. are all varying forms of protein. The human body is made up of over 100,000 different proteins, all designed to perform specific functions, much like specifically designed gears within a watch.
Proteins themselves are made from the arrangement of specifically arranged
smaller molecules called amino acids. All biological life is made from
precisely arranged amino acids of twenty different varieties. These
amino acids link up like colored beads on a necklace to form
the specific protein needed to perform a specific function.
Different amino acids, like different colors, produce
the radically different proteins needed for
life.

Scientists have been able to synthesize amino acids and proteins in a laboratory, but every time we run experiments to form amino acids, an equal number of mirror image "right-hand" and "left-hand" amino acids are produced. Yet life only uses the left-hand amino acids. All of the right-hand mirror images are missing from life. Where did they all go?

According to the big bang model for the formation of the universe, all matter was originally compressed within a tiny speck of pure energy which explosively expanded - producing unfathomable amounts of hydrogen and helium, which condensed into stars - which produced all of the rest of the matter in the universe. Yet in every experiment where energy is transformed into matter, an equal amount of matter and antimatter is produced. There has never been an exception. Antimatter is identical to matter, except it is a mirror image, i.e. whereas protons in matter are positively charged, protons in antimatter are negatively charged. Almost all of the matter in the universe is 'normal' matter with only extremely tiny traces of antimatter. If the big bang explains where everything came from, where is the enormous quantity of mirror image matter (antimatter) that should exist?

It is almost as if God wanted to make it absolutely, unmistakably, completely, undeniably obvious that the origin of both life and the entire universe could not be explained by any natural process. It is as if He chose to eliminate the expected mirror images which should be present if natural processes produced the universe. Romans 1:20 states this another way, *"For since the creation of the world God's invisible qualities - His eternal power and divine nature - have been clearly seen, being understood from what has been made, so that men are without excuse."*

The Mystery of Star Formation

Many people understand that there is more storytelling than science in the "theory" of biological evolution. The idea that random changes could transform an amoeba into a man or a bacterium into a boy stretches the credibility limit. Thus enormous periods of time are added to make the process seem more plausible. Yet all too often Christians compromise their belief by placing God into the story, i.e. believing that God "started or guides" evolution. This ignores the technical problems with evolution. Furthermore, to anyone in the scientific or academic community, "adding God" is simply not credible because they are immersed in the presupposition of naturalism as an explanation for everything. Thus belief in God's Word is undermined, the Bible becomes irrelevant to more and more people, naturalists continue to win the fight to keep the evidence for intelligent design out of schools, and we lose our children to an essentially atheistic thought process.

Acceptance of evolutionary presuppositions in the area of stellar evolution is even more common among Christians. According to Big Bang cosmology, every star is in the process of changing from one type to another type. It is similar to the tale of microbes-to-man evolution, but on a more grandiose scale. Stars are "born" as great clouds of gas collapse to ignite a nuclear flame; yet a new star has never been seen to form, and there are enormous problems in explaining how these gas clouds could collapse. From what we know of stars, the nuclear fire should burn for billions of years until most of the fuel is used up; then the stars would expand into red giants for millions of more years. After this, the star is supposed to collapse again to become a white dwarf or another type of star. The supposed evolution of an average-sized gas cloud is gas—> star—> red giant—> white dwarf.

Other stars also need to be explained, so it is postulated that larger clouds of gas follow a different evolutionary sequence. These larger stars use up their fuel faster and explode to form supernovas, followed by rapid collapse into super-heated neutron stars. Thus their evolutionary sequence is believed to be larger gas cloud—> larger star—> supernova—> neutron star (or pulsars, if rapidly rotating). Lastly, super large gas clouds become super red giants which collapse to black holes (super gas cloud—> super red giant—> black hole).

It is definitely possible that one star can change into a different form, but there is evidence that this has happened far more rapidly than stellar evolution allows - making this a stellar decay process, rather than an evolutionary process. It has been reported by ancient observers that the white dwarf companion of the star Sirius changed into a red giant in less than 1,000 years - whereas this change was supposed to take millions of years.[1] Supernovas have also been observed, and thousands of supernova remnants can be seen throughout the universe. All of these examples show a stellar decay process, not an evolutionary process.

There is definitely a huge variety of stars in the colossal expanse of the universe. There are stars of every conceivable color and composition, each with its own distinctive spectral fingerprint. There are neutron stars and pulsars, which pour out as much energy as all the stars from an entire galaxy, and are so dense that a teaspoon of their matter weighs as much as the entire earth. There are red giants which are larger in diameter than our entire solar system, and black holes which have such strong gravitational pull that light cannot even escape their surfaces. All of this variety and magnitude was unknown when David saw the few thousand observable stars in the sky almost 3,000 years ago and wrote, "The heavens declare the glory of God." (Psalms 19:1) He could not have known the incredible complexity and variety of the heavens, yet his statement is more accurate today than when it was first penned.

Why don't scientists consider the possibility that God simply created the wide variety of stars in the universe? Perhaps because they are blinded by an assumption of naturalism. Just as with biological life (where there are enormous differences between animal kinds), there are very different stars which seem to have been placed within the universe. Given what we currently know of the laws of physics and probability, it is far more credible to believe that God simply "made the stars also" (Genesis 1:16) than that gas clouds collapsed to form these glorious objects within the vacuum of space. Just as the biological world testifies to God's power, majesty, and creativity, so do the heavens above.

1. *Astronomy and the Bible*, Donald DeYoung, Baker Book House, 1989.

SKEPTIC'S ? CORNER

Gas clouds, main sequence stars, red giants, white dwarfs, neutron stars, and black holes are placed into an evolutionary sequence and assumed to be vastly different ages. They are just as likely examples of the vast variety God produced to show his majesty and creativity. The fact that they are different has nothing to do with their evolution or age. Fish, amphibians, reptiles, and mammals are vastly different but are lined up in a sequence to explain their origin by natural causes. In the same way, very different stars are lined up in evolutionary sequence in order to try to explain their natural origin. This is simply storytelling, as no gas cloud has ever been shown to collapse into a star. And when stars do change (as with supernovas) it happens extremely rapidly - not over millions or billions of years.

آجا جفمز دن بر

سلامك يكى . برشوكت وشـ ـنـ ـشمه

ايندة اسلامك يكى . برشوكت وشـ ـنـ ـشمه

ـايـه ـسـنـده

يجه بلادى جامعة اسلامه ادخال ايتدكلر

يكى

عباسيه نك وقتلرينى ذوق وسنـفا

خلفاى

The Mystery of Language

"People do not like to think. If one thinks, one must reach conclusions. Conclusions are not always pleasant."

- Helen Keller

Helen Keller lost her sight and hearing at eighteen months of age, and the rest of her life consisted of blackness and silence. Without any auditory or visual input, she became an untamed savage by age seven. Yet with the help of Anne Sullivan she learned to read and communicate, using only the sense of touch. By the time she was twenty-five, she was able to read and speak three languages - English, German, and French. Before her death in 1968, Helen Keller had become synonymous with faith and overcoming adversity. She authored six books while interacting with presidents, kings, and some of the most famous and accomplished people on earth. Language is central to human existence and it would seem that even deafness and blindness cannot prevent its development. But where did this marvelous ability come from?

The evolution explanation for the existence of language is that it developed from the grunts of ape-like creatures as they evolved into humans. Yet even the most primitive cultures have complex language systems which communicate abstract concepts such as zero, infinity, numbers, negation ("all men are not honest"), conjunction ("God made stars and life"), and disjunction ("he chose one but not the other"). Furthermore, the "most primitive languages" - such as those of Australian aboriginal tribes - are often the most complex, and modern languages tend toward a more simplistic nature in the number of sounds and words in their grammatical rules.

There are approximately 7,000 distinctly different spoken languages (many more if dialects are added). Because language changes with each generation, a distinct new language can develop within a few hundred years to the point that separated cultures can no longer understand one another. Linguists believe they can trace the roots of the common languages, such as the 449 languages in the European language group (including French, German, English, Russian, Welsh, and 444 others), back to a single source approximately 4,500 years ago. Similarly, 403 different languages in the China (Tibet region), can be traced to a similar original source. But at some point a wall is reached.

There is absolutely no similarity between the original European language and the original Chinese language. They are TOTALLY different, with utterly different origins. This leaves evolutionists with the choice of believing that: a) completely different, complex forms of communication developed from a common source without any sign of a transition, or b) extremely complex and unique forms of language repeatedly evolved from grunts in different parts of the world. Neither option explains the development of very different language types.

ديكربار چه‌سند

هند [ ] ايچون اسلاميت سراى وحكومت

دعلومنك باشـليجه مركزى وبرهمن لكك

] بـــرس [ ] شهرينى اون ايكنـجى عصرده

اودخى اوراده صنملرى كسر ايتدى

مع

آيين ارزان اولونو يوردى ، صنملر

ندو

دو

داره

SKEPTIC'S ❓ CORNER

Evolutionists believe that the distinctly different groups of extremely complex languages developed by "trial and error." They essentially believe that languages are 'accidents' which happen dozens of times in multiple places, or that one language turned into a completely different, totally unrelated type without leaving a trace of that transformation within cultures. The biblical model predicts that there should be very distinct groupings of languages with no relationship to one another. The latter is exactly what we find throughout the world. For those willing to think about the evidence, the biblical model clearly explains the evidence better; however, accepting the Bible as truth is not a pleasant choice for those who do not wish to yield to implications that they do, indeed, have a recent and personal Creator to whom they are accountable.

All of the languages in the world can currently be placed into approximately ninety very different language families. These may be further refined into a smaller number of distinct groups, but the development of these groups is still a mystery to naturalists. The complexity of languages is analogous to the complexity of very different biological creatures - lots of similarity within basic types but enormous gulfs separating the basic body structures.

Without language we would be reduced to animal-like survival activities. There could be no musing about origins, no pondering the meaning and purpose of life, no searching questions concerning life after death, and no conceptualizing of abstract concepts. Even Einstein commented that the psychology of human beings is more difficult than the understanding of physics, because without language there could be no study of physics. Language is perhaps more complex than anything it strives to represent. How could chance processes of mutations ever have developed it, in all of its complex forms?

The Christian understanding of language is that it exists because God exists. Language was given to mankind, fully formed and fully functional, at the beginning of creation. Different languages exist because they, too, were given to mankind at the Tower of Babel to slow the spread of evil between people groups. Thus very different languages suddenly appeared, showing no sign of gradual change from some common source. This is exactly what we find, and through the grace of God even a blind, deaf human can learn to speak multiple languages. Helen Keller was a strong Christian who clearly recognized Who had enabled her to overcome adversity.

DYING DYNAMO

Michael Faraday was called the greatest experimental physicist of all time. This humble Christian invented a vast array of electric mechanisms long before anyone else had even dreamed of such things as electroplating, electric motors, and magnetic induction of an electric current. So great was his contribution to our understanding of the operation of the universe that not just one, but two basic measures of science have been named in his honor (the faraday – a unit of electrical quantity and the farad – a unit of capacitance). He is the only scientist to ever be given such an honor. Yet to the end of his life this self-educated man remained a humble believer in the authority of Scripture - including the recent, supernatural creation of the universe and life. In spite of his many contributions to science (Faraday and Newton were the two scientists which Einstein pointed to as his greatest heroes and predecessors in the field of physics), Faraday requested to be buried with a simple white cross and referred to as simply Michael throughout his life.[1]

One of the most important features making life possible is the Earth's magnetic field. Without this protection, harmful rays from the sun would strip away our atmosphere and fry all life on Earth. Yet this field is decaying at a rapid rate - having lost 15% of its strength in only the last 150 years (since systematic measurements began). The implications of this are enormous. A straightforward understanding of magnetism indicates the Earth, with its solid iron core, was made originally with a very strong magnetic field which has been decaying since its inception approximately 6000 years ago. The only other alternative explanation for the Earth's magnetic field is that it is a self-generating dynamo which makes and maintains its own field.

A dynamo is an extremely complicated machine which acts as an electrical generator to produce direct current using spinning energy. Early versions of such an apparatus were used by Faraday in his work to understand the

SKEPTIC'S ? CORNER

For evolutionists, it is unthinkable that the Earth could have a permanent magnetic field (which is rapidly decaying) as opposed to a dynamo (i.e. a continuously regenerating field) because without a dynamo, the only possibility is that the Earth was recently created. Therefore, the problems finding a working dynamo mechanism are simply ignored, unrealistic assumptions are used in theoretical calculations modeling the Earth's core, and those who actually do the research assume that eventually a solution to the mystery will be discovered. Meanwhile, it is so frequently repeated that the Earth's magnetic field is generated by a dynamo (as if it were a proven fact) that even experts have come to assume that it must be true.

1. George & Julia Mulfinger, *Christian Men of Science*, Ambassador Productions, 2001, p.70-97.
2. D. Russell Humphreys, Planetary Magnetic Dynamo Theories: A Century of Failure, *Proceedings from the Seventh Conf. on Creationism*, 2013.

relationship between electricity and magnetism. Dynamos were the first electrical generators capable of delivering power for industry, and anyone who has seen the complex windings of a generator can easily see why a self-excited dynamo within the Earth is difficult to comprehend. To produce such a machine requires that undirected energy, such as heat, be turned into directed energy - such as in the form of a rotating shaft. The shaft must then drive a set of wire windings in the generator section, and "brushes" must be precisely placed to sweep against contact plates to remove current from the spinning shaft. Everything must be precisely placed and insulated so currents which are producing the magnetism are not short-circuited but directed to precise locations. For almost 100 years scientists have speculated that the Earth's core acts as such a complex, self-generating dynamo – yet multiple technical examinations of the idea have failed to explain how this could be true.[2]

The latest attempt to prove the Earth has an interior dynamo has been a ten year old, multimillion-dollar project at the University of Maryland to model moving fluids within a 10-foot spinning sphere filled with conductive molten sodium. All zones can be temperature controlled and the outer sphere spins at up to four rpm while the inner core can independently spin at up to 12 rpm. The apparatus has been fully operational since April 2012, but there has not been any indication of even the slightest dynamo generating fields. Had this been achieved it would have been world shaking news in the scientific community. In other words, every experiment has failed to support the concept that the Earth has a self-generating dynamo, while actual measurements of the rapidly decaying magnetic field of the Earth perfectly fits what would be expected if the Earth was literally created only 6000 years ago. So which theory, an ancient evolutionary Earth or a recently created Earth (as believed by the brilliant experimental physicist Michael Faraday), is based on faith and which is based on scientific observations?

Time and the Domino Effect

Isn't the idea that God created everything in six days just a poem or literary device? As long as we acknowledge God as Creator, who cares how or when He created? Furthermore, hasn't radiometric dating proven the earth is billions of years old? These, and a host of other valid questions, arise when discussing what the Bible has to say about the age of the earth.

Leaving aside the fact that the majority of dating methods indicate the earth is young and not even considering the problematic assumptions of radiometric dating methods (which start by ignoring the reality of a worldwide flood) … let's just consider the biblical implications of denying a recent creation.

The first problem is one of consistency. Almost every Christian denomination faithfully points to the Bible as God's divine revelation to man. Yet many church leaders are willing to accept almost any interpretation for the beginning of the Bible except for a straightforward reading. This inconsistency is quite apparent to the watching world.

The first chapter of Genesis describes the sequence in which God created the universe and various forms of life over a series of six "days." The original Old Testament of the Bible was written in Hebrew, and the Hebrew word for day (YOM) can mean either a single day or a long period of time. But just because the word "day" used in Genesis can mean "a long period of time" does not mean that is how it was meant to be understood. Every time a number and/or the words "morning" or "evening" are used in the Bible in combination with the Hebrew word for "day" it means a normal twenty-four hour day. Furthermore, the only one of the Ten Commandments in which God tells us why the commandment was instituted - *"[Keep the Sabbath day holy because] in six days the Lord made the heavens and the earth, and all that is in them, and rested on the seventh day" (Exodus 20:11)* - emphasizes this creation of the universe in six normal earth days. If we expect the world to accept what the Bible has to say about salvation, while at the same time undermining what the Bible has to say about creation, how credible is our message?

But that is not the biggest problem. The biggest quandary is what to do with Adam and Eve. The book of Genesis lays out concept after concept as a foundation for understanding reality. These are accounts of actual history which stand like a row of dominos to be accepted or rejected by each person viewing the evidence:

- The first domino is the recent creation of the universe.

- The second domino is the creation of man, right at the beginning of time, with mankind meant to live forever in fellowship with his Creator. The Bible starts with the summary statement, *"In the beginning God created the heavens and the earth,"* and when Jesus was asked about the permanence of marriage, He responded, *"Have you not read that **in the beginning** He made them male and female." (Matthew 19:4)* People have always been around.

- The third domino is our rejection of God's authority, which resulted in a just God bringing about death as a penalty for our rebellion. (God would later come as Jesus to take upon Himself the penalty of death which we deserve.) Not just mankind, but all of creation, was altered by our actions. This factual tragedy is known as "the Fall."

- The fourth domino is the nearly total depravity of mankind - resulting in God sending a world-covering flood as a timeless reminder of His hatred of sin and its effects. This event explains the fossils and geology of the current world.

- The last domino is the revelation of moral truth which directly follows the acknowledgement that we have a Holy Creator who made the universe with moral laws which are as absolute as the physical laws which rule creation.

Now let's look at what happens as we topple *the first domino*, while naively expecting it to have no effect on the other foundational dominos. Radiometric dating methods are used to date ancient human remains back fifty thousand years or more. (Some rock layers with obvious human remains have been dated at over one million years.) Thus, if you accept the methods used to date an ancient earth, you cannot remain logical and consistent unless you accept the same methods as proving that people have been on earth, living and dying, for hundreds of thousands, if not millions, of years. If this is true, where do we fit Adam and Eve? A million years of human history has absolutely no biblical support and makes a mockery of biblical history. Adam and Eve become a myth - simply a spiritual concept. ***The second domino has fallen.***

If people have been living and dying over huge periods of time, then it is not our actions which brought about death; it is just the way God made things. Therefore, death cannot be the penalty for our sin and rebellion; God simply made things that way because He wanted to do so. God, in essence, becomes the author of death, rather than mankind being the cause of death. ***The third domino has fallen.*** If the flood never happened, God did not cause this event as a judgment in response to mankind's sin. If the worldwide flood never happened, this event is not a viable explanation for how the earth's sedimentary rock layers and fossils formed. The worldwide flood as a judgment of sin by God simply becomes a myth. God changes from being both a righteous Savior and a holy Judge to pretty much irrelevant. ***The fourth domino has fallen.***

If we are logical, we now have a God who made everything via death and extinctions over billions of years→Therefore man's actions then have nothing to do with death and disease (i.e. God either is powerless to stop disease and death or just doesn't care enough to do anything about it)→And we can't really believe anything the Bible has to say about our origin, biology, geology, or human nature. Yet unbelievers are supposed to give their lives to this God and live by the rules of an allegedly inspired book - while this book cannot be believed from the beginning. Why not just make up our own rules of right and wrong and live according to our personal desires? ***This is exactly the situation today; the last domino has fallen.***

What is so sad is that very few people connect the rise of relativism with the rejection of our recent creation (the first domino). But this is the unstoppable result of the denial of this foundational truth of Christianity.

SKEPTIC'S ? CORNER

Many skeptics of our recent creation are actually sincere believers in Christianity, yet they have been convinced by the world that radiometric dating methods prove that the earth is ancient. Therefore, this is the filter through which they view Scripture, and they have no choice but to twist the text in order to fit in these huge time periods. There is no logical, consistent response with what to do with the clear language that God created the universe in six earth days. Nor do skeptics have a logical explanation concerning where to put a real Adam and Eve and the origin of human death into a biblical time frame of history. Thus, these sincere believers are actually skeptics who ultimately drive the very people they are trying to reach away from accepting God's Word as relevant to reality.

How Science Became Censored

Modern science is dominated by one over-arching, unbreakable rule, and heaven help any teacher, professor, student, or researcher who dares even to hint at reservations about this principle. What is this foundational assumption of scientific truth? That all reality must be explained by natural causes. In other words, the philosophy of naturalism, resting on a belief that cosmic, biological, and geological evolution are facts, is the only allowed explanation for the existence of everything around us. Hundreds of students, teachers, and professors have been fired, demoted, and kept from obtaining science degrees over the last several decades because they have expressed doubts over this dogma of modern science. Thousands more have been intimidated into silence, knowing of the repercussions, should they mention the scientific hurdles not overcome by evolution. This is how the true understanding of what science was meant to be - a study of God's creation so that we would see His divine nature revealed through what He had made - has become censored.

There is incredible irony in the oft-repeated mantra of evolution, "No real scientist doubts evolution" or "Creationists don't publish in scientific journals." Any who dare to present the evidence for creation or the problems with evolutionism are excluded from obtaining advanced degrees, teaching, or publishing papers - making this claim a self-fulfilling reality. The widespread nature of this discrimination and suppression of truth is documented in a recent book by Dr. Jerry Bergman, who himself was fired for exposing students to the problems with evolution.[1]

Censored Science has presented some of the best biological, geological, and cosmological clues that fit into the full biblical model of our origin. Does this viewpoint stretch your understanding of reality? Absolutely. Does it matter? That depends upon what you do with this "starting point" for a complete view of reality.

Since we have a Creator, we also have a solid basis for moral absolutes which do not depend upon the shifting sand of human opinions - absolutes such as: do not lie, do not steal, do not covet the possessions of others, do not lust after someone to whom you are not married, put nothing above your devotion to your Creator, etc. Since we have a Creator, it also is reasonable to believe that this physical life is not all there is to our existence. Why would this Creator end our existence forever at the moment of death? Therefore, once our physical existence comes to an end, we will someday stand before our Creator, who also claims to be an absolutely just judge, and give an account for our lives here on earth. If you have ever broken even one of these moral absolutes, will you stand guilty or innocent before this perfect judge? At that decisive moment, what is the penalty you will deserve in face of perfect holiness and justice? Breaking any moral law is known as "sin," and the Bible simply states as a fact, "The wages of sin is death." (Romans 6:23)

Every man-made and Satanic-inspired religion has one thing in common - some set of rules trying to cover our guilt and make us acceptable before a perfect Creator. Yet the moral absolutes that reveal our fallen nature - or any set of rules, for that matter - cannot remove our sin and make it possible to live for eternity with a God of perfect holiness. God the Father is perfectly holy. His very nature requires perfect justice for wrongs committed and a full payment for them. But He is also infinite in mercy and has Himself provided such a complete payment for our sin. How can this be? The Bible declares that God laid on His Son "the iniquity of us all" who then paid the debt in full. God's Son became human and took the penalty we deserve so we would not have to be cast out of God's presence for all eternity. The Bible also says that God the Father has given all judgment, that is, the role as judge, to His Son. It is Jesus, the Son of God, to whom we will give account for all that we have done. It is as if the judge in our trial stepped down from the bench after we had been declared guilty and offered to take the penalty we knew we deserved.

The Bible can be trusted when it talks about physical things such has the origin of life, the reality of a worldwide flood, the sinful nature of mankind, the origin of language, and the age of the earth. It can be trusted when it talks about the pathway to peace and fellowship with God. This path is simple, but in no way easy, because it involves acknowledging our self-willed approach to life is wrong and our being willing to heed God's prescription to healing and redemption.

To return to fellowship with our Maker we must acknowledge that we have broken God's moral absolutes and have no way of repairing the damage. Second, we must accept God's gracious provision for our sins - that Jesus Christ died in our place - paying the penalty for them in full. There is no other way to come back into fellowship with God - if there were, Jesus would not had to die on the cross for our sins. He also rose from the dead to prove there is victory over death. All of the death and agony in this world is the result of our sin, yet Jesus paid the price for that sin. Only by accepting Jesus as your savior will you discover a quantum shift in perspective on reality, priorities, and eternity.

The danger of an absolute adherence to the principle of naturalism (upon which scientific thought currently rests) is that no amount of evidence concerning biblical truth will convince a skeptic who is committed to the presupposition of naturalism. Yet God has made the truth readily apparent (see Romans 1:19-26). The most important reality is not the evidence for creation, but what we do with the ultimate truth of all history - *"For God so loved the world, that he gave his only begotten Son, that whosoever believeth in him should not perish, but have everlasting life."* – John 3:16

1. *The Slaughter of the Dissidents*, Dr. Jerry Bergman, Leafcutter Press, Aug. 2008

Bruce Malone has 27 years of research experience with the Dow Chemical Company. He has a BA in Chemical Engineering from the University of Cincinnati and holds 17 patents for new products with Dow. In 2008, Bruce retired to work as full-time director of Search for the Truth Ministries with the vision of "Awakening Hearts and Minds to Biblical Truth". Search for the Truth has printed and distributed over 500,000 books, primarily to students and prisoners. *Censored Science* is his fourth book dealing with the evidence for creation.

Bruce travels widely and has given over 1000 presentations on the scientific evidence supporting the reality of our recent creation throughout schools, churches, and universities in 14 countries. He has served as an adjunct speaker for the Institute for Creation Research and is an associate speaker for Logos Research Associates. Bruce and his wife Robin have been married for 32 years, have 4 children (Michael, Marc, Margaret, and Matthew) and five grandchildren (Corrie, Eleanor, and Lily, Elliot, Violet). They reside in Midland, MI.

SHARE THE TRUTH AND SAVE!

Science & the Bible

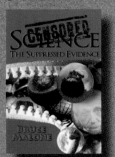

Is your science being Censored? Learn about how science actually confirms the Bible's account of creation.
128 pgs
Full Color
Hardcover

Evidence for Creation

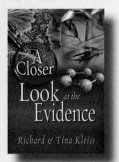

Scientific evidence for creation for every single day of the year. A daily devotional.
408 pgs

History & the Bible

Learn how history from all over the world points to and supports a biblical timeline.
128 pgs
Full Color
Hardcover

Daily Devotional

Illustrated sequel with MORE evidence for creation. An article for 365 days! Beautifully designed.
408 pgs

Any 1 book = $12   2-9 books = $9/ea.
10+ books, $6 each!
(mix & match, priced to give away)

Resource	Qty.	Cost each (see above)	Total

Return order form to:

Search for the Truth
3275 Monroe Rd.
Midland, MI 48642

or CALL
989-837-5546

SHIPPING:
1 bk. add $3, 2-9 bks. add $2/ea., 10+ bks. add $1.50/ea.

Subtotal	
MI Residents: add 6% sales tax	
TOTAL ENCLOSED	

SHIP ORDER TO:

Name: _____   Phone: _____

Street: _____

Town, ST, Zip: _____